The Seven Steps of Leadership Journey

OrangeBooks Publication

1st Floor, Rajhans Arcade, Mall Road, Kohka, Bhilai, Chhattisgarh 490020

Website: **www.orangebooks.in**

© Copyright, 2024, Author

All rights reserved. No part of this book may be reproduced, stored in a retrieval system, or transmitted, in any form by any means, electronic, mechanical, magnetic, optical, chemical, manual, photocopying, recording or otherwise, without the prior written consent of its writer.

First Edition, 2024

THE SEVEN STEPS OF LEADERSHIP JOURNEY

SYSTEMATIC LEADERSHIP DEVELOPMENT TO STAY TALL IN THE TURBULENT TIME

LAKSHMI NARAYAN PANDEY

OrangeBooks Publication
www.orangebooks.in

Acknowledgement

I am immensely grateful for the unwavering support and inspiration from my family, friends, mentors and loved ones throughout the journey of crafting this book on leadership and personal development. Their encouragement has been the driving force behind the completion of this project.

First and foremost, I extend my heartfelt gratitude to my parents, whose endless love, sacrifices, encouragement and values have shaped me into the person I am today. To my brother and Sisters, whose camaraderie has added joy and warmth to my life, thank you for being a constant source of motivation. My deepest gratitude goes to my wife, Shalini, whose patience, understanding, and encouragement have been my pillars of strength. My extended gratitude to my father-in-law and the entire in-law family.

I am thankful for my daughters, whose innocence and love have been a grounding force, reminding me of the importance of the lessons shared in this book. Your future is my greatest motivation.

My special thanks to my friends from SASTRA for continuously upgrading my resilience, my lovely friends of my village, My Colleagues, and my professional mentor, Dr. R. Vasu.

In conclusion, I express my deepest thanks to all those who have played a role, big or small, in shaping this book. Your collective influence has been invaluable, and I am humbled to have you all in my life.

With gratitude,
Lakshmi Narayan Pandey

Contents

Acknowledgement v

Chapter - 01 1
The Seed of Discovery: Why Leadership

Chapter - 02 16
How and What of Leadership

Chapter - 03 33
The Inner leadership

Chapter - 04 67
Leadership Quality Development

Chapter - 05 106
Leadership System Thinking

Chapter - 06 134
Leadership Implementation

Chapter - 07 152
Brand Leadership Management

Chapter - 08 166
Conclusion

Chapter - 01

The Seed of Discovery: Why Leadership

This beautiful evening was perfectly ready to welcome the top management of Innovation Xtream at Silicon Valley of India Bangalore. Amrit and Astrid were excited about this town hall meeting. Innovation Xtream is one of the few leaders in technology advancement and clients across the globe in the Internet of Things & Blockchain domain. The time had come to an end when clock ticked at 18:15. Energetic and passionate technocrats were waiting eagerly to listen to Christopher. The vibrant town hall, beautifully decorated with knurl-shaped lighting, had a perfect blend of vibrant minds.

Good evening, leaders, in your immense contribution and support, we are the fastest-growing future technology organisation. There are two ways to reflect your success of light: to be the candle or the mirror that reflects it. I am glad to see both sets of colleagues. Before starting my presentation, I would like to thank the board of directors who persistently contributed to the growth strategy, and that is developing the one among the rare team of leaders. Hall was full of the claps. Mr. Christopher projected the annual revenue and status of each segment; he presented Corporate social responsibilities to uplift society, and then, with full Conviction, a roadmap for next 5 years was presented. Question and answer session was amazingly superb, and the town hall was commenced to end with a commitment from Mr. Graham Christopher to meet in next global meeting in Paris.

This was the time for Chatting over coffee; Amrit, Swedish lady Astrid and John were discussing yesterday's mind-blowing session. There was a long-discussed dream without any plan to start a training consultancy to develop leaders. Their joyous moment was turned into silence by an email integrated into their Mobile phone, Mr. Cristopher- a goodbye message to colleagues. It is unbelievable that a person who was presenting the vision of company just two days ago, presenting long-term targets with conviction, talking about next generation's leadership. Was he a leader or an actor? Astrid questioned.

This is the genuine question Astrid asked; John replied, at workplace, we see every day a new commitment without a clear road map. We see managers mentoring colleagues as a responsibility to develop leaders, leaving next day organisation. Even in broader sense in society, in sports, in education, in communities and sometimes, we as individuals start some impactful activity to change around, to contribute, to lead with action, but all these disappear after a few months. Someone starts again freshly and never loop closes. A leader, a torch bearer, a mentor, or a guide is required to avoid chaotic motion at all level or a system must be in place to work irrespective of the change of individual. The secret of success is consistency of purpose. If consistency of purpose is in place, why leadership and what is expected from leadership will be clearer with a question mark. Can we develop leadership skill? If yes, then how?

Amrit made a fun respectfully, John, you throw the question like flow of water, and they turned into smiles.

Astride was still serious - Can we have a brainstorming session on leadership? We had to play a vital role in our society. We cannot leave a few basic questions without addressing them. They all agreed to discuss it the next day.

Amrit attempted to set the boundary of discussion. What shall be our scope of discussion?

John replied gracefully; this will not be certainly limited to specific to any organisation. We have a lot more experience in our lives where we grow. We have seen a lot of people gaining genuine respect, transforming the others' lives. Materialistic success alone cannot be the only criteria of our discussion. We had always imagined to gift to humanity through our new start-up. Every century, humans have gone through transformation through invention, which, in a short span, have impacted the lives of millions. Be it discovery of electricity, flying crafts or internet, but we have not evolved in centuries that "What are the ways and means to transform all individuals in this gifted world?" How each one of us will be leading for a cause of co-existence and bringing up each other? The brain-storming session started and continued for a week; they presented scientific data from various research organisations to summarise the interpretations. Now, the conclusion was really a path-breaking one.

Why Leadership:

"Leadership is not about being the best; it is about making everyone else better." - Bill Gates.

The data from Organisation for Economic Co-operation and Development revealed the time spent on different activities per day by the people of different countries. This data is originally in minutes spent per day, which is converted in years by the analysis Team. Looking at the most productive 50 years of use throws the bigger picture on time, which is the most valuable asset of ours. If we convert that data into 80 years of human life, an average Indian spends the time given below. Surprise to the further, the similar data from the US Bureau of Labour Statistics is in a similar pattern.

	Actual data (in Min/day)	Converted in Years
Paid work	272	9
Studying	25	1
Sleep	528	18
Social care/ Volunteering	44	2
Housework & Shopping	160	6
Personal care	75	3
Eating & Drinking	84	3
TV & social media	252	9

Table 1.1-15-64 years the most productive 50 years taken here, 1-14 years as early life and 65 to 80 as senior citizens not included in this

Looking at this bigger picture in the most productive time of humans, further categorising essential time which cannot be altered.

- 39 years are essential for Human beings, which include sleep, paid work, housework and shopping, personal care and eating and drinking.
- 11 years are only productive time of 50 years which we could have spent and distributed in the purpose of life, family, and friends, transforming others and self.
- In these 11 years, also watching TV and social media takes our 9 Years.

This data surprised all the three; John nailed further ooh my god, for all the reasons of being human, we spend only 2 Years' time.

You are right, John; surprise is even ahead.

- These are average data for working employees, sports persons, the divine communities called community helpers, farmers, or any activities which take more than average time will heavily skew this data. It may end up in 6 months to 1 years' time for the real cause of humans.
- If we do not make a healthy, trustful environment or we do not like the job, we waste an average of our valuable 9 years of human life.

Now, I feel it is our utmost responsibility that

- To make an honest effort to optimise these 11 years of time for the purpose of life, family, and friends, transforming others and self.

- To make the realising management, society leaders, business owners, and productivity consultants who claim tough task masters for number game that just providing a conductive work environment they are contributing valuable 9 years in every human.

A few practical observations show that we have seen a lot of success stories, but ultimate success is like a wave which has many ups and downs. During these successes at any level in this world, we do not see the sharing of reason along with how to handle the given situation of intermittent failures.

Even at our work, schools, and society, we start our activity with do and do not in the beginning, but when we grow, we have to manage our activity as well as managing things which we have to learn from our experience; no one teaches.

Let me clarify with a little explanation: When we join an organisation, we start with formal training on how to do our daily work. After a certain time, we start managing team, but no one teaches us how to handle failure, decision-making process that evolves over a period, time management, and how to boost team's productivity. These leadership skills cannot be acquired through training; these are processes. It comes from consistent daily basis of effort. How do you start being comfortable with challenging discomfort? How do you understand and respect the pros and cons of your team? How do you support to unblock the stuck situation? Your response is also being evaluated by your surroundings. Hence, the only way to develop leadership is truly a genuine effort and enjoying the process. Humans are not machines, but the sorrowful part is that even machine has some defined guidelines to improve productivity, but we do not have them. Take a little big picture of our observation of farmers; for centuries, the agriculture sector has been almost in same place with little scientific advancement in real sense. We have well-developed labs, research centres and scientists. We see challenges of water and global warming. After using fertilisers, we have challenges to go back to organic without impacting productivity, but we do not have a mass implementation because we do not have leaders adequately in this sector to drive this journey. Same is with other sector organisations.

Leadership is learnable Skill:

"Leadership is not about being born with certain qualities; it is about acquiring the knowledge, skills, and mindset necessary to inspire and guide others." - Warren Bennis.

Many of us think that leadership is a natural talent, but after studying great leaders Mahatma Gandhi, Mandela, Benjamin Franklin, the Wright brothers, Einstein and other people, they evolved over period. They were keen observers. They learnt from the voice of their inner core and voice of the market. Two things were widely common that the question they arrived at, the inner voice or People's Voice as problem appeared to them, they never ignored. They attempted to find the solution to the best of their capacity. Second common thought is they firmly believe that if they cannot lead themselves, they cannot lead others. Leadership in itself cannot be self-proclaimed unless a set of people or users will not be getting benefitted. **Breaching the gap between your self-leading capability and approval of people who benefitted from a good cause is called leadership.** Think about Wall Disney; he was fired from a newspaper for not being creative, his Micky mouse got rejected with controversy of being Anti-Women, and three little pigs were rejected, stating four characters are not fit to commercialise, but Wall Disney had both qualities. He had a problem-solving attitude, so every time he found same answer from his self-doubt and remark raised by people that it will succeed. Second, he led by leading himself. He did not give up on his rejection, and today, Disney is one of most the reputed in entertainment world. These leaders were not born; they faced rejections, they learnt from their mistakes, they believed in self, and they achieved.

Universal Iceberg Principle:

Iceberg Principle, where 10% are tip of Iceberg and 90% are submerged in water is more scientific than statistically better accepted Pareto principle in which 80% result can be achieved with 20% of the effort.

Leadership Skills are more vital nowadays because it has huge potential to be discovered; it is believed that only 10 % of leaders, whose contribution and Process of turning into leadership is Known, but 90% of leadership qualities are not known as similar to iceberg.

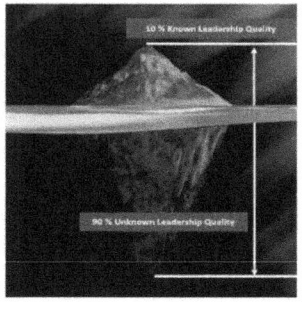

John had a question: Why these 90% of parts are not discovered? Do you have any Idea looking at Amrit?

Amrit attempted to explain, there are various reasons; we mostly know political leaders and great inventors and leadership is understood as only subject to imagine as someone as authority, but actually, we all are leaders of our life. We all are contributing to leadership; these small yet significant contributions on a daily basis are very important to encourage. Do you not think that a milkman who ensures milk for society in all weather and in all situation at morning are leaders, do you not think a boy distributes newspaper in the morning are not leaders? Firefighters who are ready for safe rescue of people leaders, a Soldier, leaving behind family posted in dangerous forests of South Africa and in Syria as peace keeping force, not a leader. Of course, money alone is not a factor for these services; they do not take this as job, they take it as a service without realising it. Encoded natural ability of human potential gets activated in those people, but we never thought systematically to study them and their service-oriented thought process, which required horizontal deployment. This is far better diffusing because they relate to the common man, and this way will develop the view of gratitude.

Leadership is not only important for Individuals, Communities or society but even important for nations. The four most important aspects of leadership:

- Result-driven system of leadership comes from inclusive, open-mindedness, transparent and diverse societies.
- These qualities, ones practiced in society, each individual at a certain level starts imbibing and same

Will be transferred to next generations:

- A leader definitely steers and takes organizations, communities, societies or Nations to next level. The basic ideas of all books, training, Personal development and self-help coaches to focus on

Developing good habits, Team building skills, staying fit and authentic, relationship building, continuous learning and inspiration, etc., because individuals as bricks of organization, societies and Nations can transmit these positive vibes to people and situations around you.

- Clearly, leadership is not about having all the great qualities, but the one aspect of leadership is to manifestation of strong love, compassion and transformation in people around you without compromising on principles.

Leadership is an important aspect that can be seen from the book, "Why Nations Fail" by Daron Acemoglu and James A. Robinson. These examples explain how important leadership plays a role in prosperity.

Extractive Institutions in Zaire (now the Democratic Republic of Congo) under the leadership of Mobutu Sese Seko have seen extractive institutions, characterized by a small elite that monopolizes political and economic power. It hindered the national growth, quality of life, and led to high inflation and massive human rights violation. Political power was enjoyed by elite group close to power. He ruled 32 years before seizure of power in Kinshasa on 17th May 1997. In his regime, he had the support of great democracies like USA, France and Belgium. He had the support of the Chinese government. In spite of all privileges and access to a well-developed system as a leader Mobutu failed to understand.

It is not the strongest of the species that survive, nor the most intelligent, but the one most responsive to change. This is a classic case study of disaster in a state due to a lack of quality in leadership.

The second example is Comparative Analysis of North and South Korea. In the same book, writers Acemoglu and Robinson explore the contrasting experiences of North and South Korea, two nations that emerged from a common history but adopted different institutional frameworks. They argue that the extractive institutions in North Korea, coupled with a lack of political and economic freedoms, have resulted in economic stagnation and widespread poverty, while South Korea's more inclusive institutions have contributed to its remarkable economic development.

Now, see some data due to differences in leadership quality where South Korea has a presidential and multiparty system whereas North Korea has a dynastic dictatorship.

- South Korea has lopsided GDP of 2 trillion-dollar in comparison to North Korea's 40 billion dollars.

- North Korea has life expectancy of 69 Years, whereas South Korea has life expectancy of 79 Years. Leadership and Inclusive society do increase your lifespan.

- Per capita GDP of North Korea is 1700 dollars, whereas South Korea has 39000 dollars.

- Your consumer behaviour is also, to a great extent, driven by leadership; North Korea has 3.6 million cell phones, whereas South Korea has 61 million.

- Your acceptance in diverse world has also a deep-rooted relationship with your leadership; as per Lonely Planet, North Korea gets only 10000 tourists per year, mostly from Chinese nationality, whereas South Korea gets 17.5 million visitors per year from across the globe as per world data.

SUMMING IT UP:

➤ You have very little time in your life to contribute to a good cause. We have to learn to use the time we spent very carefully.

➤ These Three friends, John, Astrid and Amrit, represent all of us and try to find **Why** leadership?

➤ Leadership is a learnable skill and only cannot be known by training. Leadership starts with your action and effort to confront the challenges.

➤ Leadership is not about great Business tycoons, self-help writers or political leaders; they are only 10 per cent. 90% of leadership lies in people who are part of our day-to-day life. Starts putting subtle observations around 90% to learn and implement in your life.

➤ Leadership is all about bringing the change in lives of people, Societies, Communities and organizations around you for a good cause.

> Why leadership? Because humans, by nature responsible to support, contribute, and create systems for a better world. Individuals, Societies, Communities, Organisations and Nations have a clear and close relation to efficient leadership skills.

> Breaching the gap between your self-leading capabilities to approval of people who benefitted from a good cause is called leadership.

PRACTICE YOUR UNDERSTANDING:

- How can I bring more meaning and Value addition to the people around me?

- What steps can I take to live in alignment with my truest self and purpose each day?

- How can I observe the good quality of people around me and implement my purpose?

- Why is leadership important for you? Write in your journals in details.

- Write the 5 greatest people you know personally who admire you as a leader. What quality do they pose?

Chapter - 02

How and What of Leadership

The Journey of Leaders:

This was the first meeting to plan the way ahead of a new venture. They decided to meet a consultancy leader who is considered to be the best corporate trainer in Bangalore to understand the depth of the problem. Understanding the problem better is the key to finding the best solution. Mr. Aarav was the CEO of the consultancy "We Transform Life". He had a genuine passion to help the people, but he had a certain Niche and he wanted to restrict urban class management leaders.

All three met Mr. Aarav in a beautiful park called Atal Bihari Park in CV Raman Nagar, an area named after Scientist CV Raman, and park was named after the Ex-prime minister of India. Mr. Aarav cheered them saying, I called here to this part of Bangalore in this park to give a first message - "Leaders have a life even after death", indicating the board of two greats in their Karma Bhoomi. What is this Karma Bhoomi - Astrid asked.

Ooh, sorry dear, Mr. Aarav replied, it is the field of expertise.

Your mission is bravo. I read your primary finding, and my observations are in sync with you.

- Time is the most un-optimized subject, which shall always be looked at a bigger picture
- Leaders are not born; only children are born.
- 90% of leaderships are unknown; hence, the virtue of leadership is yet to discover in a bigger sense.

I will refer you to a great man known to me who can help you in this mission. You get ready to travel to Varanasi. Varanasi is a crazy city; I love it- Astrid said.

Mr. Aarav Asked -Have you visited ever? Astrid replied - No, my Mom and Dad met first time in Varanasi. I have beautiful memories in my home even today.

Mr. Aarav said, lovely, nice to hear girl. Continuing on the subject, Mr Sri Swamy was my mentor when I lost.

He has masterfully built up his chain in defining new dimensions of leadership. Mr. Aarav gave the contact details and address, introducing him gracefully.

Mr. Aarav Said, you have taken a great work on your shoulder.

I would love to share my experience. He repeated again; Leadership is learnable skill, but practice is key to mastery. This is only one skill that can bring the ultimate goal of human life: Enduring happiness and fulfilment.

Awareness on leadership Qualities - How it works?

Mr. Aarav continued; Leadership is a quality that works against common wisdom. Once, in an Interview, one of the richest people, Mr. Bill gates, was asked who was richer than you.

He named with beautiful example of a newspaper vendor who had a shop at Airport. It became two times in his business trips that he took a Newspaper but could not pay him back because he had 1000 dollar to exchange and vendor did not have change. Bill Gates is the person of expressive gratitude, so one day, he purposefully found him and wanted to gift him something bigger for giving him free newspaper. Vendor rejected and said, Sir, I gave you a newspaper when you had no option to pay even though you had money. Now, you are paying back as the richest in world but I respectfully deny it. This money cannot be as precious as the moment you needed a newspaper, and I offered but I do not need money that you are offering. **The value of giving and taking depends on time**. I am still relatively poor in materialistic money but richer by heart.

The man to whom Bill Gates said, Richer was lucky enough because Bill Gates was aware of his strength. Money could not buy his leadership quality of customer service. Both situations are available everywhere in our Societies and organizations. Many leaders in our society are not aware of their strengths to have expressive gratitude like Bill Gates. Many of our corporate clients know that their employees, support staff, vendors, and customers have virtues like the newspaper vendor but do not want to admit it. They learn and consolidate these leadership qualities from them but perhaps do not have courage to admit, like Bill gates that someone is richer than him due to service-oriented mindset. These two things are quite obvious.

This is how leadership starts working.

But why are leaders not aware of the Strengths, John asked?

They are afraid of their personal losses, dear John; business will lose some of the most productive people, and services will lose some of finest art from which few individuals are benefitted. Leaders know that good is enemy of great. Turning good to great is a risky process. So, those true leaders keep themselves good.

This has a two-dimensional thought, where one believes and conceives the idea to achieve what truly they deserve; second, when someone is not aware of his qualities or is lost in the way. They need someone to throw the light in the darkness to wake up; only the torch bearer is required in this second category. The rest game of accomplishment will be taken care of by an individual.

How and what of leadership Execution -Example by Mr. Aarav:

Gandhi and Mandela are considered the greatest national leaders in India and Africa respectively. The one thing that made them different from all contemporary leaders is the ability to create awareness. They had a people-oriented approach to involving and creating more leaders, a chain of networking, created compounding impact on the goal as well as a long-lasting influential personality.

In fact, our predecessors had the art of standardising the best practices. That is the reason all our traditional agriculture had a standardised practice sink with weather and starting to finishing the process of agriculture, the way they store those food items...etc. Either Mahatma Gandhi, Mandela or our old practices of farming made things simplified. This is what leadership does. **Leaders make things simplified**. The solution offered on involvement and easy to understand; how to do it? Now, from decades back, trying hard to attempt the modern way of farming, rather than producing and pushing to market, produce what is required in market. But we are stuck because the way of creating mass awareness to develop the leaders in each village, each city, and each tribe is far challenging.

To be precise, in each home -Amrit spoke, excellent Mr. Aarav.

You are right, Amrit, Growing the chain of leaders with synchronised ideas of change for the betterment is the gap now in the system, and we must find a way to fill this gap.

Leaders develop a thought process to address the gap of mass impact.

Astrid asked a question: **What** did you teach your corporate clients to bring the thought process of leaders?

Very good question, Astrid, Aarav appreciated it. We teach them about the "Power of Regret": A technique like window, in which people may see the shortcoming in future.

Power of Regret:

Let me share a fact about one of the courageous human efforts in history. In 1950, Vietnam descended into civil war. It had two ideologies; one was pro majority people, friendly social reformist Viet Cong predominated in North Vietnam, and other was Diem with very fringe support on the ground and predominately in South Vietnam. The most powerful and equipped with modern artilleries, the victorious USA decided to support South Vietnam. This was strategic loss of USA, where they withdrew forces. Vietnam was united; it was the worst humanitarian crisis after the World War, but how a tiny Vietnam shook the system of the most powerful nation. The base was made on the pillar of our previous discussion, "the awareness of Vietnamese pride", which was laid down by communist leader, visionary and social reformist, Mr. Ho Chi Minh.

But the real cause was using the most powerful technique to improve human is "Regret". Lesson learnt and action on those weaknesses that caused the regret.

Bringing back your attention, Astrid, the feeling of regret is very powerful technique where we learn from the mistakes of others or ourselves in the past. North Vietnam had a long history in war; they fought successfully against Japan from 1939 to 1945 and defeated the French in the war between 1946 and 1954. Vietnam, did it? -Amrit asked in surprise. Yes, my friend. This is the power of synergy. They utilised **the lessons learnt** by warriors turned into leaders. They understood the ground difficulties faced in the villages of Vietnam; North Vietnamese army truly supported them but masterfully applied the technique of regret, explaining to them the impact and cause of these difficulties, those Japanese and French who occupied our motherland. If USA comes to our land, our generations will face even the worst conditions. Army arranged workshops even in remote locations to create awareness of what we lost during different wars and how our generations are impacted. The power of regret united the people of North Vietnam to fight back against the mighty USA, and Vietnam achieved the biggest victory, eliminating line 17 between North and South. If we apply power of regret like Vietnam in our day-to-day life, against our visible and invisible challenges, then how do we do this? Let me tell you about the survey by our team, Mr. Aarav was in flow.

Here are the 10 biggest human regrets in the later part of time when they grow as senior citizen. These are the reasons which could have been managed and achieved with little or no investment. Which I am sure will be taken by the mentors of leadership in the journey of evolving skill to develop leadership.

Ten Regrets of Human in later part of Life:

The earlier the regret, the better is the result. Writer Daniel H Pink says in his book, "The Power of Regret, that when we handle regret properly, regret can make us better. Understanding its effects hones our decisions, boosts our performance, and bestows a deeper sense of meaning. Regret makes us human. Regret makes us better. Regret sometimes gives us a sense of purpose.

- I have not spent enough time with my growing Kids, ageing parents, adorable wife and lovely siblings.

- I was neither committed to teaching the core values to my kids nor became a person of value to my parents.
- I spent much time in my shallow, worthless job without realising the productivity.
- I did not take care of my health due to unhealthy habits.
- I was not courageous enough to express my feelings to my loved ones, Colleagues and Mentors.
- I was not ethical at some moment and did not behave with humility
- I would have been happier and enjoyed life in each challenge; my fears were fake.
- I often sought society's approval.
- I would have met my family and loved ones' expectations in a better-organised manner.
- I wasted my life without creating any social Impact.

These 10 regrets have one thing in common; they are not about becoming the richest or the best in world in anything. This does not demand a big investment of money and energy; it is all about not channelling human traits systematically.

Time is the only resource that is most limited; we do not spend time with our loved ones and spend too much time in non-value-added activities that are not worth deserving. How many times do we call our sibling and memorise the special moments of childhood? How many years ago we sat near our respective parents full of gratitude and could express that hey, Dad, I miss you so much? When is the last time you hugged your adorable wife with the same excitement as you met first? When was the last time you put your hand on your kid's head with remorse, hey, sorry dear nowadays being busy -I could not play with you?

How many times have you spoken with your leader expressing, boss, these are the areas I feel we should work together to achieve greater efficiency.

Remember, expression is like paint on the wall; it keeps relationship shining. Be courageous enough to be expressive. Be aware that if you are not expressive in your relations and loved ones, how can you be expressive in Society, at work place and some bigger public speaking forum.

Leadership is based on relationships built with trust, hope, love and encouragement. Leadership journey begins from Home:

Once, Mahatma Gandhi said, that Health is real wealth and not pieces of gold and silver. A healthy attitude is contagious, but don't wait to catch it from others. Be a carrier for your family, friends, and loved ones.

Next, regret areas are largely categorised as habits which were acquired rather than naturally encoded. Not being ethical even in the case no one sees pain in an individual's conscience. Even the slightest lack of ethics and deviation from human-oriented behaviour will never bring you happiness; people harm more to themselves than others. This will reinforce your fulfilment at the time of the incident as well as long time. Henry Ford, the revolutionary who dreamed of the car for every American, once said -You can take my factories, burn up my buildings, but give me my people, and I'll build the business right back again. The last regret is more deeply with social nature of humans, which actually does not necessarily require a bigger resource. To create a social impact, you need not be required to be ultra-rich or to be called a philanthropist. You require energy and willpower.

Ask yourself, do you require money for:

- Community support,
- Good conduct and courtesy
- Skill sharing and Kindness campaign
- Guiding the children from less privileged
- Donate Goods like used books, cloths, etc.
- Support for the elderly

Amrit, John and Astrid looked into each other's eyes.

Mr. Aarav was in flow to explain this powerful technique beautifully. He added, even the most successful people often had a predominate regret from this list and tried to contain it.

Sachin Tendulkar is a legendary cricketer in India who is regarded as "God of Cricket". It was his farewell speech with tearful eyes that had millions of messages, a life-transforming for leaders. He expressed gratitude to every family member, from his sisters, Father, Mother, Aunt, and Brothers to his wife and Kids, expressing regret for not spending quality time with them. This is the bible to think and act on the most important aspects of your life where even owning the reward of God with satisfaction of huge success could not stop to regret what he lost.

But just think for a moment; you are working for an organisation that might not have a culture to give you a moment to regret publicly, sometimes not even a farewell, which at least you deserve.

Read each word, trying to quote what I have written in my diary word to word on 13th November 2013 from None other than great Sachin Tendulkar:

"The two precious diamonds of my life are Sara and Arjun. They have already grown up. My daughter is 16, and my son is 14. Time has flown by. I wanted to spend so much time with them on special occasions like their birthdays, their annual days, their sports day, going on holidays, whatever. I have missed out on all those things. Thanks for your understanding. Both of you have been so special to me that you cannot imagine. I promise you that for 14 and 16 years, I have not spent enough time with both of you, but for the next 16 years or even beyond that, everything is for you."

Astride asked, admitting the importance of working on these lessons learnt from our elders. Have you worked in this area where people benefitted, Aarav, Mr Aarav? It is OK, Astrid; you can call me Aarav. Yes, our team has advanced to some extent, but as I explained, most of our clients are corporate, so working on time management to balance their lives is an important requirement.

Leadership is not about never failing; leadership is using the power of regret around you available, leadership is about effective use of lessons learnt, leadership is about good management of bad experiences.

The Wheel of Life - Learn to Turn:

The one thing was clear to our solution provider team based on learning human regret and understanding the lifestyle of clients; the allocation of the time and disparity in life to respond must be balanced. If the wheel of life is to turn to keep moving, there shall be all turning efforts in the same direction. Let's explain this scenario.

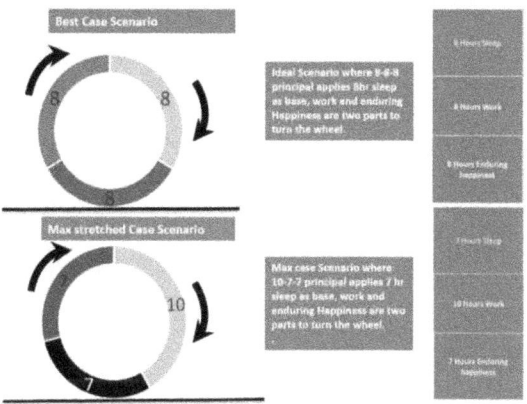

We must play between these two boundaries, John, for avoiding all these regrets and our enduring happiness, which has many factors, will not depend upon a solid time distribution only where a range of work shall not exceed 10 hours per day and time of sleep and Happiness hour shall never go below 7 hours per day. Vital is to integrate work and Happy moments, and the time till which I define these enduring happiness hours; let's call them personal hours.

What is this integration? Amrit asked. This is a good question, Amrit; Integration is being yourself. We are misaligned because we are acting as two persons in work place and in private time. We try to look cool; we try to play diplomatic; we do not feel empathetic to our colleagues. We do not respect individuals; at least many of us do not love our jobs and in private life, we expect ourselves to love and be caring to loved ones. It is not going to happen; your life is like wheel and torque shall be in one direction. Your thoughts, your actions, your behaviour aspects shall not be different, and if this will be different, the disparity is reason for all shut of anxiety and stress. If you try to blame your boss for everything, then no reason that you will not blame your wife. If you never guide or mentor your subordinate, or colleagues, then for sure, it is nearly impossible to teach core values to your kids. This is the one aspect of integration of your commitment, action, thought and behaviour.

Is that another aspect of this, Mr. Aarav? John Asked

Yes, Dearest John, that is final brief from my side on your leadership journey; all the best to you all. Let's remember these golden rules in journey.

- Leadership is not a destination; it is a lifelong journey of growth, learning and inspiring others to reach new heights.

- You need leadership quality because in the journey of leadership, you will be paved with challenges. Your qualities will help you navigate through.

- As a leader, remember that the journey is just as important as the destination. Cherish every step and mind the legacy you leave behind.

- Leadership journey requires resilience, adaptability and the courage to navigate unchartered territories.

To elaborate on the golden rule, leadership is a continuous process of development. Input is more important than results. You attended some great training or acquired a good position does not make you leader. The way you communicate and behave with your people and situation makes you a leader. How beautifully you present numbers does not make you a leader, but how you perceive intangible numbers like trust, synergy, catching aspiration and creating an acceptable culture make you a leader. You cannot measure these intangibles like how much trust, how much love, and how much synergy. But it exists because you approach your colleagues to debottleneck the situation of conflict. You bring the trust to the team because you help someone if he/she is stuck without passing judgement on competency. It exists because you wake up in the morning, make a nice coffee and offer on bed to your wife before she wakes. These are processes every day and every moment you have to breathe to be a leader.

SUMMING IT UP:

➤ In the journey of leadership, every leader must be reminded that **the value of giving and taking depends on time**.

➤ Leaders make things simplified.

➤ Power of regret is a technique used by great people in the journey of leadership. This regret must be learned also from other people.

➤ These 10 regrets have one thing in common: They are not about becoming the richest or the best in world in anything. This does not demand a big investment of money and energy; it is all about not channelling human traits systematically.

➤ Leadership is based on relationships built with trust, hope, love and encouragement; Leadership journey begins from Home.

➤ The wheel of life must be balanced in the 8-8-8 rule, but even in maximum range scenario, work shall not exceed 10 hours per day, and time of sleep and Happiness hour shall never go below 7 hours per day.

CHECK YOUR UNDERSTANDING:

➤ Have you ever witnessed the value of time in your life?

➤ What was your response to manage?

➤ How do you express your gratitude? Write the ten most valued relationship in your life. Meet or call them and truly express what you feel about them.

➤ Write your regrets of life, share if it is possible, with meaningful social media, collect the details from others' mistakes, and apply powerful technique of "Power of regret".

➤ Monitor your Wheel of life for 1 month and find out how much time each day you spend in all three categories: work, Sleep and Enduring happiness. Try to balance this important Leadership learning.

Chapter - 03

The Inner leadership

This was not only Journey of three Colleagues, College friends and genuine leaders, but also a journey of transformational system "The Seven Steps of Leadership". The Road trip from Delhi to Varanasi was well-planned. India is developing an amazing Infrastructure; John and Astrid are looking at Agra Expressway. We must stay tonight in Agra. We will see the great Taj Mahal.

It was a beautiful evening in the corridor of the Taj. I salute the people of India and their architecture. These white Marble and reflection of waterways are self-relaxation.

This Taj Mahal has the potential to be the most self-relaxing place in the world. It was an overnight journey to Varanasi. We were well received as per the arrangement communicated by the Mr. Aarav. It was a well-arranged guest house with a narrow entry for our hired car, and both sides of the narrow pathway were decorated with flowers and different variety of Basils. Left part of the guest house had a big Banayan tree and a big cow-shed. Right Part of the guest house had a big Bungalow that had a few guests of different ethnicities. Between the Guest house and Bungalow, there was a small traditional home, made of wooden and soil-like structure and a man with smile, looking vibrant, in ordinary saffron attire yet magically impressive, was sitting. Swami Niwas -Amrit read the Sanskrit letters.

After little Rest and refreshment, especially Basil flavoured energetic tea, it was time to meet our Mentor.

We were surprised that our mentor was the same person we saw with some extraordinary shine on his face in saffron attire. Swami entered and greeted us like we had known for years. The Indian sages are well known for their gifted Human-Connect skills. Astrid mumbled.

Did you all come directly from Delhi Airport or have some rest in the journey? Swami asked with very calm and relaxed posture.

"We saw the Taj Mahal," John replied.

Welcome the leaders of the future; you all half learnt.

Enjoy each step of the journey rather than only enjoying Destination- That's what you did, guys. It is awesome.

Some of our finest work comes through discussion with others. These are the reason we are highly socialised folks. Mr. Aarav told me about your mission of developing leaders in societies. This is the much ignorant area. Different researches indicate alarming data at work place and in society. Let me add some more points in your discussion paper, **why leadership** is important -Swami swiftly shifted to the subject.

- According to Wrike's United States stress statistics from 2019, 94% of American workers report experiencing stress at their workplace.
- Gallop's new data on global workforce in 2021

Suggests that 7 in 10 people globally struggle and suffer due to work place environment.

- A private survey organisation, Automatic Data Processing, conducted a survey in European countries and found that 18% of people endure stress at work place **every day**.

Editor's choice data of USA article says in 2019 that

- Depression leads to $51 billion in costs due to absenteeism and $26 billion in treatment costs.
- Work-related stress causes 120,000 deaths and results in $190 billion in healthcare costs yearly.
- According to Times Job survey of over 1500 working professionals across India, 80% said they feel stressed at work place, and out of all stressed people, 60% said the reason is their leaders.

Now, you can understand how leadership is important. As a leader, you have responsibility for the Company, societies, communities and people around you. You cannot afford ordinary life. You must have some special skills so you can least harm your surroundings. As a human, even though unintentional, you cannot afford the being cause of stress, death of people, depression, relations issues, accidents and whatnot. Then how do you see yourself in the mirror when you get up and ready at work place?

Great leaders don't see themselves as great. Great leaders see themselves as human:

Stress, anxiety, inhuman treatment, and unfair practices are more dangerous than Crime, Terrorism, etc. Every country had some well-laid mechanism to handle crime and Terrorism but overlooked the human aspects, which cause more harm, which is far outnumbered by actual data. Even the most developed nations overlooked these aspects. This is the one biggest reason we need the science of human potential amplification, purpose of human, learning and implementing from nature and evolving the leaders throughout societies. The concept of leadership is very simple: **you are on board as many possible people for good cause and mutual growth physically, mentally and spiritually**. In the North-East state of India, there is a village called Mawlynnong; this is the cleanest village in Asia. How did they achieve it? They made it ritual; everyone in the odd 600 people of village turned into leaders, and they passed on this transformation from generation to generation. Even today, when they turn into tourist spots, they take this responsibility to educate others respectfully to follow this. **The leadership is all about the art of transferring, transforming and building an ecosystem**. How is the today's tech city and one of the world's wealthy, and prosperous place, called Silicon Valley, transformed? The brand leader and dean of Stanford University, Fred Terman, envisioned the dream to set up the finest stretch of technology in California's San Francisco. He inspired the outgoing students to set up their own companies around Stanford Universities. The wealth of universities was invested initially in funding. Just imagine the confidence and drive of transformation. How many of B schools not only teach them how to do business but their own wealth also invested in selected companies to their own aluminise. Very rare because either they are not convinced of solidness of skill they transfer into learners or they do not believe in the business idea that they teach. **This is the big disconnect between the reason on which they are founded and what they are actually doing**. Same is true for Technical and Engineering universities.

Amazing thought Swami ji - John supported the way of thinking. Yes, John Fred Terman convinced Bill Hewlett and Dave Packard to open the HP, the way, ecosystem and support process of Aluminise were connected through universities and the leadership.

They supported each other in funding and evolving business thoughts of technological aspects without violating copyright. His effort paid off in 1958 when SBIC Act was implemented as a major support to private investors. Today, world's all great organisations like Google, Facebook, Hewlett Packard, Apple, Oracle, and Adobe have head offices in Silicon Valley. Almost 18000 tech companies are established by Stanford University's Aluminise; their annual revenue is over 3 trillion dollars. **If Stanford University had been a nation, they could have been the 6th wealthiest country.** Starting a business in Silicon Valley as Alumina is great edge; even today, they maintain the standard. Investment-friendly ecosystem can be heard with millions of investments during the Coffee chat. Blue Bottle is a place, where every day, investors just used to wait for vibrant minds. This is one aspect, but the impact of the people who are using Google, Apple, and Facebook has a reach in every corner of the world. This is what leadership shall synergise the ecosystem.

This Synergy to evolve each individual is a key to leadership. It is embedded in each culture, but we do not realise its importance. This Synergy is reasoning that today, Paris and Milan are famous as fashion hubs, India is famous for Meditation, Spirituality, diversity and spices, Switzerland for watches and chocolates, and Japan for electronics and discipline. All these are manmade ecosystems where not an individual but a complete society shall be regarded as leader. To create leaders who have the Charisma of transforming society, like Fred Terman and Mahatma Gandhi who made the independence movement as people's movement and evolved into some of the finest leaders in biggest democracy in the world. The Villagers of Mawlynnong, who made it the cleanest in Asia is systematic and organised process. This mission, I am already running to the best of my capacity.

Astrid wanted to get clarified; Sri Swami, you wanted to teach us to turn society or individual altogether?

Sri Swami smiled with Calm and composure, I understood and studied your complete mission, folks. This powerful Seven-step technique is to transform individuals who will have synergising abilities in society. Our ultimate goal is to create leaders and impact the lives of millions to utilise human potential at the best level. You have to make some journey to mentors, which I have assigned for the Seven Steps.

Amrit had a question -Sri Swami, if these steps are created by you, why aren't you the best person to teach.

You are right, Amrit, but my mission is to democratise the art of chiselling leadership skills. This show must go after me or without me. We must be the change we wish to see in the world; this is the only reason I have assigned these leaders to support you in your journey.

The other two benefits are that you will learn a unique way of explaining these steps, which will give you variation in your mission. The second most important benefit will be networking.

Now, I will define your schedule for this fantastic journey. We all are leaders in our lives, dear, but how effective we are and how we are turning into brand leader is defined in these seven stages.

John Asked a question, what is Brand Leader Sri Swami, Sri Swami - Sorry from my side, folks, we will discover the meaning of brand leaders in our journey.

Seven stages of Leadership evolution:

I would present here Seven steps of Leadership Evolution.

All Successful and unsuccessful leaders will fall in the range of these seven steps. The difference is that Successful leaders knowingly or unintentionally follow the steps in the right sequence. Stepping out of any stage will leave the voids in you, and practicing each stage systematically will make you an excellent outlier. We, the leadership club, have a compelling vision, a comprehensive plan, relentless implementation, and manufactured talented people working together. This is a great opportunity to collaborate with great leaders and get sharpened like Iron sharpens iron. The Great Alexander said "I am not afraid of an army of lions led by a sheep; I am afraid of an army of sheep led by a lion." Follow the discipline to turn into a leader. He who has never learned to obey cannot be a good commander.

Seven Steps of Leadership

It's good that two steps are in the way by you people in right sequence; you started as the First step "Why Leadership."

Second step is How and What of leadership was equally important. With your brainstorming session and discussion with Aarav, you have put first things first. These steps, one and two, are strong foundations where monuments of leadership will be placed. There are two mistakes one can make along the road to truth**; not going all the way and not starting.**

Third step, **Inner leadership -Self Organising,** will be starting right after 2 days of warm-up stage, and I will be your mentor. The mentor of your **Fourth step** is Susamya; she is very fantastic lady. You have to travel to deep southern part of India in Thirumalaisamudram. It is situated in the National Highway 67.

The **Fifth step** is leadership System thinking, and your mentor is Mr. Hudson in Zurich. He is a farmer and nature lover; an excellent human being. You all will enjoy this journey with him. The mentor of **Sixth step** is Herald Trump from Nogales Arizona. He is the coolest guy I saw during his 6 months stay in this Cottage. Connecting the last dot, we will together explore the **Seventh step** - Brand leadership Management at Varanasi in the same cottage. It is a real minority category of Humans in this world.

The Journey of Change:

"The secret to change is to focus all of your energy, not on fighting the old, but on building the new." – **Socrates.**

Folks, few rituals in this process, we can achieve together; please involve yourself fully. Travel together and do not delegate this responsibility. All right, John committed from the Team.

It was amazing evening in Varanasi, the same air which was inhaled by great sages and the greatest spiritual leaders in this one of the oldest cities in the world. They saw various divine places on the bank of the Holy Ganges; such a vibrant energy, especially the kind of spirituality they observed upon request by Sri Swami during Ganges Aarati (The Revering to the Ganges). It was the utmost respect seen to nature in any part of world. Astrid said.

Inner Leadership - Self organising:

The best leaders are those who understand that their power flows through them, not from them. -**Kenneth H. Blanchard.**

Connect your body, mind and soul:

The first warm-up of our inner Leadership was Morning Yoga session at Assi Ghat "Subahe Banaras", where hundreds of people joined us. It was a really different calmness and energy level after performing Pranayama's different postures and breathing, especially Sun Salutation.

The inner calmness during Yoga was the discussion of the day; we really felt the calmness, and we were feeling connected to ourselves. We consulted Sri Swami after lunch, Astrid said, we all had an altogether different feelings, the feeling of gratitude, the feeling of belonging, the feeling of being rhythmic; is this some sort of black magic which I often listen to when I was in Switzerland?

Yoga is a Science of Wellness, Astrid; it is a natural process. Rather than explaining in details, I will give you some of the key thoughts which you all will think of as leader.

- When we all get angry or panic, we breathe more than normal, so our Breathing changes from one state to another as per emotion; if we can control our breathing pattern, we can control our emotions.

- Breathing rate has a considerable impact on Lifespan. Yoga increases the quantity of Air, decreases the number of breaths and increases your lifespan. Each breath is deeper and more conscious. Below is the relation between breath rate and lifespan.

Animal	Breath Per Minute	Life Span (in Year)
Tortoise	2 to 4	200
Whales	4 to 6	165
Elephant	5 to 12	80
Man	7 to 16	75
Horse	12 to 15	50
Sheep	16 to 34	25
Cat	20-40	22
Cow	25-50	20
Mouse	90-250	3

- Yoga gives a perfect balance between your body, Mind and Soul - your wheel of life to rotate in one direction must be balanced.

- Our yoga mat is a dress rehearsal for real life. How we act while on the mat is a mirror for how we will handle both negative and positive experiences in our lives. When we learn to stay present on the mat, we learn to stay present in the office. When we choose to open our hearts in Camel Pose, we begin to show a touch more love and kindness to those in need. When we sit with our discomfort on the mat, slowly, we begin to sit with our discomfort in our lives - and then we can understand why it's there in the first place. And our Ego? When we begin to let that go, that's when powerful transformation can really happen. Don't roll up your yoga practice with your mat; instead, take it out into the world and live your yoga every day!

- Yoga Plays a vital role in sequencing Sympathetic and Parasympathetic nervous systems, Sri Swami said, with reference to various research papers explaining.

- We all Human have an inner wisdom; we know what is good and what is bad but our action is not attached with inner wisdom

➤ We fall in anger, jealous and Judgement

➤ Our habits, ego, and Materialistic competition are not controlled

➤ Our Food habits, even with brutality on animals, Laziness, and Senses hurting each other, are dominant.

➤ Our Integrity, Happiness, Gratitude, everything pledged to earning money.

- So, why our inner wisdom does not control our action? Because there is no bridge between inner wisdom and day-to-day actions. Yoga is that bridge.

- Yoga is the only oldest practice, discovered by Indian sages, still in its purest form. Many barbaric uncivilised groups attacked to this prosperous nation. They destroyed our centre of education, temples and the centres of spiritual enlightenment, but yoga is the only practice that made them realise to preserve even without their will. Today, it is practiced and gaining popularity in more than 152 nations attached to science.

It was an amazing session to understand the benefit of breathing, different postures and Meditation in our lives.

We decided to practice this every morning. We had listened only about different healthy practices, either physical, and at some extent, relieving stress and anxiety, but this touches every dimension of our life.

Next day, morning was very important; we all were ready for morning Yoga.

4P 3D 1C method:

Sri Swami arrived to place of designated learning Centre. Sri Swami had Four Jars that must be made of some environmentally friendly material, as the logo was indicating. Each Jar has three Partitions and Cap separately. We were already thrilled about today's session.

We all greeted Sri Swami with smiles in the energetic Posture of warriors, which was learnt today during yoga session. You will definitely succeed in your life, young folks. You all are quick learners. You have definitely impressed me with the way you adjusted to the cottage, with vegetarian food, the Natural lifestyle of cottage and most importantly, the Yoga mat. This is the right path towards enduring happiness because you want to spread joy through creating a leadership environment, so first you must have joy within; then only, you can distribute it to others. They all looked at each other. They never thought this. Sri Swami continued showing outside, looking at the joy of the person feeding the cow and goats; we saw the gentleman, who helped us settle in the cottage, was offering food to animals of the cottage. He is a true leader; he takes care of all the guests of various ethnic backgrounds, their choices of food, and plan of their journey; they all are so happy with him. Animals love him; they start crawling just by looking at him. You will rarely find him without a smile. He started studying now with sole purpose of better helping the guests; he has only mission to art of giving to society. He feels that he has abundant to give to society; he never felt scarcity within. He does not mind what he shall get from this world but focuses on what he can offer. This is the great value encoded in him, Swami ji explained. Astrid second it.

Now, with this beautiful example, let us start the powerful step to awaken inner leadership. This method is called **4P 3D 1C** method. They all looked at each other. What does it mean, Swami ji? This is the short representation of complete steps. He now put forward on table those 4 Jars; P represents these Jars which are universal steps; whether you are writer, sportsman, Manager, or social influencer, for everyone, these are the steps. Ds are the specific actions to your selected functions, and C is very simple yet very significant, called the Success quotient. Now, this is very simplified. They all carefully Looked at it; there were some Golden-colour words written and pasted on Jars, on each section inside the Jars and then on the Caps. Organise your life around your ideas in these simple steps, folks, and watch them come true. First comes thought; then organisation of that thought, into ideas and plans; then transformation of those plans into reality is the process which is the smoothest process against the common wisdom. Sri Swami stressed these words with an enlighten face.

Astrid asked with eagerness, Sri Swami, can you kindly explain these magical abbreviations?

Amrit supported in an enthusiastic tone, yes, Sri Swami.

Sri Swami continued with Mindfulness with a smile on his face and kindness in continuity, this is nothing magical, young folks.

It is all Practice. The Power can be created and maintained through daily practice and continuous effort. Knowledge is the only image in the mirror and practice creates a real person standing in front of mirror. This is reverse process. So, here are your much-awaited steps for 4P 3D 1C process.

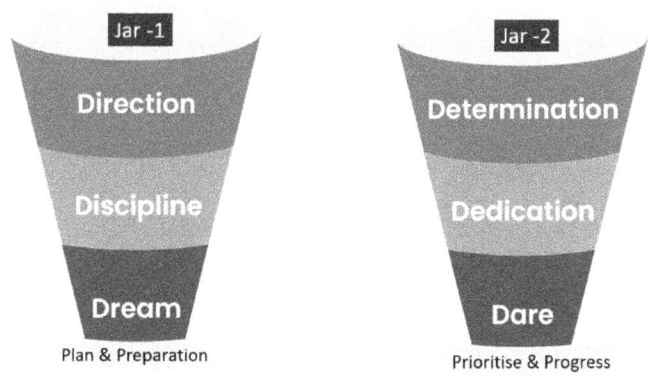

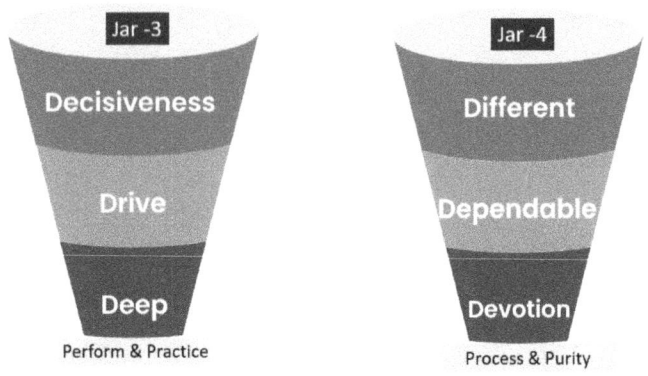

Perform & Practice Process & Purity

Sl No	Universal Steps (4P)	Specific Actions (3D)	Success Quotient
1	Plan &Preparation	Dream	Consistency
		Discipline	
		Direction	
2	Prioritise & Progress	Dare	Consistency
		Dedication	
		Determination	
3	Perform & Practice	Deep	Consistency
		Drive	
		Decisiveness	
4	Process & Purity	Different	Consistency
		Dependable	
		Devotion	

Plan & Preparation:

It was the morning of 13th June 1999 in Kargil, India. The commanding Officer of Rajputana rifle sent a radio-scripted message to Lieutenant General Mahindra Puri, Sir, I am on top of Tololing. This was the crucial advancement by the Indian Army, fighting against the enemies of Humanity. This was the Point 4590; the causalities of Indian side were far more than any other mission in the Kargil war. Indian Media criticised this as a Suicidal mission; the main reason behind this was **Plan and Preparation**. Reason could be various, but Risk assessed to achieve this mission. Resources required to support the mission were miscalculated in planning and preparation phase, but once this crucial win in world's most difficult mountain warfare thrilled the great Indian army and risk was assessed, the next Point 5140 was successfully completed with precision. The same Indian media was filled with pride of gallantries of our warriors.

Planning and Preparation shall be done with precision, and it is one of the steps of your inner leadership of each individual to contribute, even if it is done as a team.

Some of the best examples of Planning and Preparation are:

- Marshal Plan - popularly known as European Recovery Programme to rebuilt Europe after

World War II and a stable economy of Europe along with humanity-based democracy.

- NASA's Apollo 11 moon landing.
- Sir Edmund Hillary and Tenzing Norgay's Mount Everest win.

The specific actions to have a robust plan and Preparations are Dreams, Discipline and Direction. There is no hierarchy in Dream, Discipline and Direction. All three are equally important, and this is one reason that a well-Planned Dream fails without Discipline, a well-Planned Dream and a well-Disciplined journey fail without direction. The better the alignment between these three, the greater the results are.

Now, we often talk about Goal, but dream has far deeper meanings, and our Goals in life are subsets. So, the best way to set the dream first before goal and Dream can be set by clarifying Why. Goals are part of a Journey like climbing a mountain, which required actions; Dreams inspire you, and Goals Change the life. Dream defines you, and Goal defines your commitment; Dreams stretches your vision, and Goal stretches you. The only thing is the one vision, the one thought you often meet with in you, which solves the purpose of life; after achieving that, your life is complete or start sustaining that Dream. Every day changing scope and imagination of some phony ideas is not a dream.

For example

- Elon Musk has Dream to build cities on Mars
- Wright brothers had dream of flying in Air
- Martin Luther had dream that a white and Black kid would play together one day.
- Common Man dream for well-settled Kids, Happy retiral life.
- Some people dream of helping society or less privileged.

Now, this ultimate dream must be fragmented into small actionable process that is Goal. Goals where two things will happen; one, you will be taking action in a defined timeline; second, you can verify the direction. Breaking down goals into small steps to achieve dreams shall be done in very systematic way.

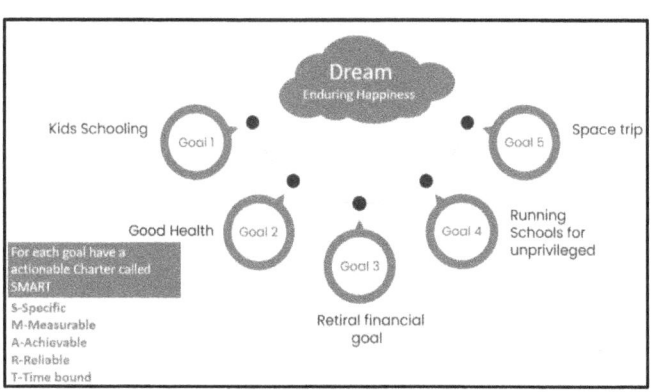

The Goals are defined from the main ultimate dream; this goal shall now be Specific, Measurable, Achievable, Realistic and Time-bound where ever possible action plan.

Astrid asked a question, we have listened a lot about SMART goal setting; is it possible in all cases?

Not possible in all cases, Astrid, Vasco De Gama and Wright brothers were not set the SMART Goal. The Goal is more related to your spiritual quotient, but we are very much comfortable with numbers, so SMART is practiced.

Another important aspect is Discipline; it is about self-discipline, commitment and ability to stay focused while adhering to the plan. It includes your bedtime to early morning rise time, preferably anywhere from 4:30 AM to 5:00 AM. Yoga will help to put you in these disciplined schedules. To be Disciplined, you have to follow the rules of nature. When we were children, we were not expected what to do, but for our safety, it was expected what not to do. In our lives also, we are now focused on to-do list, but our focus shall shift on not to-do list and adhering not to do list itself will ensure discipline as remaining. Discipline alone can represent the wheel principle; each activity of yours shall be aligned in organised and systematic rather than random.

A few examples of disciplines:

- Continuous learning
- Time management
- Focus on health and wellness
- Financial discipline

We must remember that discipline is not about adhering to all conditions, it is not robotic process;

most things break due to lack of flexibility, and discipline also follows the same. I am not talking the core value but the scheduled activities; you have flight in an early morning, 5 AM, which is your yoga time. It is obvious that you have to skip the yoga. Discipline shall never be taken over by Procrastination. This is the completeness of discipline, but this is not the meaning of discipline that I will never change a set schedule. It is more about intent rather than strictness.

Direction has two senses here; one is when you chase your dream through your actions and efforts, all these resources are put into right perspective, how would you know? The second sense of Direction is setting the process for successor; these two steps define the direction. Now, take an example of mountaineering. For Mount Everest, there are eighteen identified routes from various origins. That means people have tested success to summit at Everest. Each route is incomplete direction. Out of these eighteen routes,

Two routes are the safest.

- South-west Route from Nepal side
- North ridge from Tibbets side

These two Routes have 4 and 6 base camps, respectively. All other routes together have 25% causalities. Out of 4 mountaineers, 1 is dead. Now, this is the complete direction. Mountaineers know less risky routes; they know the tested base camps where they can track their progress and milestones. They know the specific risk area and method to follow even in these two routes. This is now the complete direction.

Now for transformation as a leader, it is always the best practice to understand Risk and way you have to go. To start with take reference of successful process, modify it to make your Mote, Define the milestones and track the progress at definite intervals continuously.

All Three were amazed at the first part of this lesson; they repeated it.

For universal step - Plan and Preparation is the sequence of specific actions, Dream, Discipline and directions are fantastically impactful.

Sri Swami smiled with calmness with deep breath, yes, folks; thanks for the encouragement.

Astrid asked, Sri Swami, you also need encouragement, being master in the skill of leadership.

Even God needs encouraging words, Astrid, by the way if you believe in God. Without us, no one will offer regard to God, and without God, we assume that No world will exist; so, we worship. Without going into complexity of scientific and unscientific, only take the beautiful lesson of Encouragement of humans to God and again feel gratitude with true trust that we all are due to him. Now, move on to next step.

Prioritise & Progress:

We never have enough time to do everything, but we always have time to do the most important things in our life and process of Choosing the most important with right resources is prioritising. Action on these Priorities is progress.

There are various prioritising techniques developed, but none of them is naturally fluent; one among the very frequently used in corporate is Eisenhower's Urgent and Important categorisation. This will definitely not work in creating great leaders in every field. You see the man, taking care of cattle, and the guest of cottage does not know any modern prioritising techniques, but he rocks in happiness and performs the activities in such an organised way that many CEOs keenly watch him to take some inspiration. So, how exactly would he be prioritising his activity? This is the Simple Task storyboard mapping technique. You know your daily routine; after Completing morning fresh up, we Practice Yoga and meditation after light breakfast, and then we go for our respective work. If you look at our first 2 hours in morning, all cultures and ethnicities are dedicated to Health-related brackets. Now, from 8 to 5 PM, we do our activity for earning wealth as well as our reflection of mental and spiritual health with other co-workers. In the evening, we return home and spend time with family and friends and take rest. So, in very broad sense, our daily habits are itself prioritised in broad sense. These priorities are:

1. Health of yours and Family Members
2. Your absolute best at work place
3. Quality time with near and dears
4. Rest of your body and Mind in sleep

Now, make in your Mind the first filter to direct the work in only the bracket to which it belongs. For example, if you want to teach your Kids a new skill, to play badminton and watch entertainment show, arrange the work order in Basket 3, Quality time with Nears and Dears. This is the ancient wisdom of folks to prioritise activities.

The limitation of the Urgent vs. Important arrangement of modern era is- who decides urgency? What decides importance? Often urgency is defined by others, and importance is defined by some sake of need. In all these processes of urgent and important war, one person going to be unhappy; that is, you. It is not your actual prioritisation; it is Imposed Prioritisation.

Now, in Priority and Progress, specific actions are Dare, Dedication and Determination. All these are equally important, and do not have a hierarchy.

Dare is often discussed in a more positive sense as Courage; this is the single most common characteristics, which is either misunderstood or ignored in leadership development process. Let's try to understand the fact of leadership, which has an immense content of dare as leader. Nikolaj Vavilov was born in a small rural Village in Russia. He saw the famine in and around him. This had a determination and dedication within him, deeply rooted to counter. Nikolay Vavilov turned into a great geneticist and plant geographer. He studied the food ecosystem across the globe. He started the mission of all Humanity to finish Famine from Russia and across the world. He conducted successful experiments in genetics breeding and concept of super-food for multiple-time productivity without impacting the vital elements of foods. It required great courage at the time; everyone had a mission to be a defence scientist or growing industrialisation. He listened to Farmers across the world. He envisioned the Vavilov Institute of Plant Industry, where all the collection of Seeds, Super Seeds and Breeds developed for his mission to counter the Famine was stored. This vision was uniquely transferred to his co-workers and colleagues of institute and today, it is an example of professional courage. It was time of World War II; in September 1941, German forces sieged Leningrad, all the supplies, including food supplies, to the city. The scientists and Team of Nikolay Vavilov in Vavilov Institute of Plant Industry were not thinking about their life. It was the time when Nikolay Vavilov was in jail in a forged conspiracy case, which was proven later to be false case. In the absence of a leader, the whole scientist sacrificed their lives. They had a rare category of seeds, high production capability of breeds, and rare food-producing ecosystem elements. It all could have been food for them for a year, but they buried in the tunnel safely all these seeds for executing successful "The mission of humanity". They all died with hunger but did not touch a single seed which was collected to fight with famine. The diary recovered from the site later revealed that they were firm, dedicated and determined that the purpose of the mission was to save humanity from famine, not ourselves, so save these rare breeds even at the cost of their lives.

This world is full of such great examples, folks; **Dare is the quality of mind, heart and soul** that enables a person to face difficulty, danger and pain without fear. Generally, daring is understood to hurt someone, to be resistive, but in actuality, daring is a rare quality which encourages to do what is right for society rather than individual. In our society, in our nation, in organisations, and in our communities, we are not able to throw many superstitions and mediocrity and adapt to change for betterment because of lack of courage.

Lack of courage even makes you lethargic, procrastinating and mediocrely successful.

The simple technique to practice dare is always stick to the purpose of the event, and purpose of process with intent of betterment for a bigger cause rather than selfish individual.

The Scientist of Vavilov Institute of Plant Industry had that deep-rooted purpose. Just practice the connectivity from head to heart, that is 18-inch theory. Courage for leadership is important because, without it, it is not possible to practice any other virtue.

Dedication is again connected root, which is Quality of Commitment. Think about the quality of commitment of Nikolaj Vavilov; he was able to transfer the same level of commitment to colleagues on Mission of humanity. How did he become engross in this commitment and it was from childhood. In fact, in reverse, the quality of your commitment is dedication and firmness of purpose that is determination, comes from your why. Create a strong why, empathise with society and communities, engross in their problem, and rather than criticising problem, take the solution, the closer one to your chest. Stronger is your why; the frequency of your why and courage to think and take the first step make your strong Dedication and Determination.

Perform & Practice: Perform and Practice is vital step in inner leadership because here we encode the techniques within us to get a better version of self.

The specific steps are here Deep, Drive and Decisiveness. Uncommon to other specific actions, there are sequences, which we shall practice.

A strong **Drive** leads to a **Deep** understanding of a subject, which in turn can transform the ability to make informed **Decisions.**

Drive is an internal force that propels individuals to take action to overcome challenges and to achieve the desired outcome. This drive comes from a strong sense of purpose, which is your why. It is chain reaction; when you have strong drive, most likely, you will invest time and resources to understand the level of complexity of your functions like an old hand. Which means your approach is Deep. Now, both Drive and Deep individually and being combined enhance your Decisiveness which is a very important functional aspect of Leaders. With your high drive, you are striving for a desired result, and for that, you must make a quick and forward-moving informed decision. Deep understanding gives you choices to make the best possible decision in given circumstances.

Process & Purity:

Different:

Innovation: Effective leaders often demonstrate the ability to think differently and encourage innovation in their teams and organisations. They look for new approaches, solutions and ideas to meet challenges and opportunities.

Creativity: Being different can mean approaching problems with creativity and originality. Leaders who foster a culture of creativity and diversity of thought can inspire their team members to offer unique perspectives.

Dependable:

Trustworthy leaders are consistent and reliable. They keep their commitments and can be trusted to keep their promises. This credibility builds trust between team members and stakeholders.

Stability: Trusted leaders provide stability in times of uncertainty. Their constant presence can help calm anxiety and create a sense of security within the team.

Devotion:

Devoted leaders are often deeply passionate about their vision, mission or purpose. This passion is contagious and can inspire others to share their dedication and commitment.

Leading by example: Devoted leaders lead by example, put in their work and dedicate to achieve their goals. When team members see their leader's unwavering commitment, they are more likely to follow suit.

Now, take the example of Elon Musk,

Elon Musk (Tesla and SpaceX):

Different (Innovative): Elon Musk is known for his innovative thinking in the fields of electric vehicles (Tesla) and space exploration (SpaceX). He revolutionized the automotive industry by popularizing electric cars and has ambitious plans for colonizing Mars.

Dependable: Musk has consistently pushed the boundaries of technology and delivery timelines. He has demonstrated dependability by meeting milestones, such as launching the Falcon Heavy rocket and delivering electric vehicles that meet or exceed their promised specifications.

Devotion: Musk's dedication to his vision of a sustainable future and space exploration is unwavering. He has invested a significant portion of his wealth and time into these ventures, even in the face of numerous challenges.

4P 3D 1C process is the strongest base of all giant structures of leadership. Practicing and imbibing this powerful technic will put you on the journey of a brand leader.

SUMMING IT UP:

➤ Enjoy each step of the journey rather than only enjoying Destination.

- ➤ **Why Leadership** is again explained in a unique way with data on how unsafe and unfair work places and societies are impacting human life.

- ➤ Leadership deals with People, so they have a strong influence on life; they must have special skills.

- ➤ Every country and Society has mechanism to deal with Crime, but impacting a significant amount of life with Skills is responsibility of leadership across globe.

- ➤ The inner leadership is 3rd step of leadership, and first action is to keep yourself healthy. Connect your body, mind and soul.

- ➤ Breathing and Yoga is ultimate method for your overall health, longevity, and emotional balance.

- ➤ 4P 3D 1C is a strong action roadmap for developing inner leadership.

CHECK YOUR UNDERSTANDING:

- ➤ Kindly write a few examples where you find the impact on people or system due to leadership.

- ➤ Write in your regular journal about your Health focus.

Like a Morning health ritual.

- ➤ Draw a framework of Plan and Preparation. Integrate the Dream, Discipline and direction.

- ➤ Try the framework for all 4P 3D.

- Think and write 3 good practices which you do consistently.
- Write your dream in your journal and split it into Goals.

Chapter - 04

Leadership Quality Development

"If you want to be a leader who attracts quality people, the key is to become a person of quality yourself."
~ *Jim Rohn*

The journey begins in a verdant haven from Chennai to Thirumalaisamudram, where ancient trees whisper wisdom to eager souls. Sun-dappled trails lead to great educational sanctuaries, SASTRA University, where curious minds gather like leaves in a gentle breeze. Here, streams of knowledge converge, flowing through vibrant classrooms and open-air amphitheatres, where lessons harmonize with birdsongs.

Each step unravels the secrets of the natural world, revealing ecosystems teeming with life.

Biotechnology gardens bloom with vibrant diversity while observatories unveil the cosmic ballet overhead. The scent of old books in library mingles with the earthy aroma of moss-covered stones, creating an ambiance of intellectual enchantment.

In this symphony of nature and education institutes, Susamya had her cottage, the place where hearts find resonance and spirits soar on wings of discovery.

After a brief visit to the surrounding, we discussed the schedule of our learning and decided to start at 7:30 AM next day.

Leadership Quality Development:

Susmya started after greeting us as Hello, Trailblazers. Questioning is the root of all solutions, and Leadership Development is no exception. Leadership development without having Leader's quality will be occasional and not consistent. What is the fun of having a superior exterior design of a ship without Quality of sailing in all conditions, including Heavy storm in the ocean. The purpose of the ship is not to have glossy look but the robustness of keep sailing for an entire lifetime. This inbuilt arrangement is Quality of Ship. Similarly, look and exteriors of humans are not sustainable and cannot give transformative results. The purpose is to strengthen the fort of the soul to stay strong in all the storms of life. The utilising and grooming are inbuilt qualities which all of us have but are not able to acknowledge. Shall we humans fear challenges? The answer is that you must not. A baby who was born emerged as a super winner much before coming into existence. Out of 100 million sperm, the healthiest one travels to Fallopian tube to fertilize the egg. That is how humans come into existence. Think about the win of musical chair among 100 million that we all live humans have crossed. Here, I will tell you folks about self-questioning technique that clears your self-doubts and put you on the path of Leadership Quality Development.

Have you ever thought about how did Mahatma Gandhi, Martin Luther and Nelson Mandela achieved success by leaving behind widely accepted principle?

Widely accepted thought is a loop of Purpose cycle.

Have you ever thought about how Ratan Tata, Head of White House USA, Elon Musk, and such people manage their activities yet end up managing some time for social cause?

Widely accepted thought is a loop of Productivity cycle.

Have you ever thought about how Super Performers like Sachin Tendulkar, Versatile Super Lady Babe Zaharias, and Major Dhyan Chand achieved this unbelievable footprint?

Widely accepted thought is a loop of Leadership Habit Cycle.

Have you ever thought why Warren Buffet, Birala family, Mukesh Ambani, and many successful family ventures focus on Family values transfer to next generation?

Widely accepted thought is a loop of Self-Balancing Cycle.

Leadership Quality development is a long-term process, but the identification of areas where each section of our society, Industries, and Community leaders shall work to improve is short-term. This short-term may be subject to periodic review.

John asked, Susamya, can you put forward the meaning of these questions in an organised way? Susamya Nodded yes; perhaps she sensed the complexity.

4 steps x 3 depth of cycle: The Summary of Leadership Quality development is in 4 steps, and each step has 3 sub-steps. Leadership development is a systematic process, and after analysing thousands of Successful Leaders, we observed the approach. For Example, the Purpose cycle is first step to getting a clear and strong foundation of leadership. To understand the Depth of the purpose cycle, we must focus on finding validating and aligning purpose. This can be done with consistent working, not only overthinking and planning. This process of continuous working is called the **activation of the leadership gateway.**

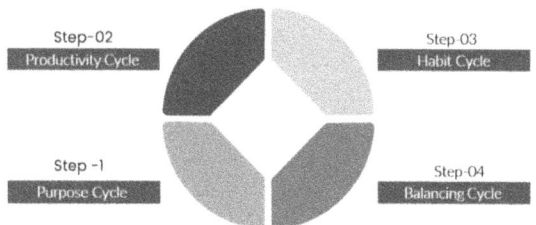

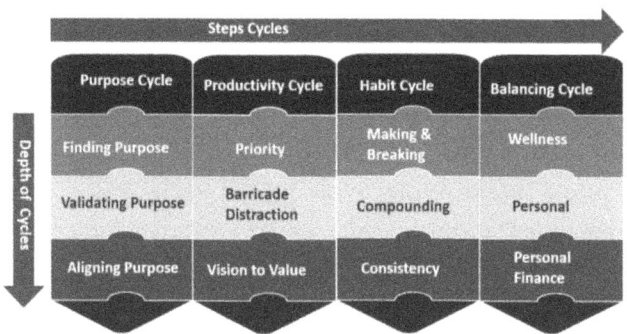

1. Step 01 -Purpose Cycle:

Set the Purpose and Align the Purpose:

As per GDP per capita, African Nations like Somalia, Congo, Burundi and Liberia are among the lagging countries. The reasons on various scale have been analysed by economists and Polito-Psycho analysts. They came up with various reasons predominately like,

- Colonising effect
- Geographical locations
- People are Diverse in small groups

- Leadership crisis

On these parameters, if we asses these countries, we find that none of the above comes too close to logic. Many colonial nations across the globe have done extremely well, including two vibrant democracies like USA and India.

Japan and Indonesia, such countries, have progressed well in managing geographical disadvantages. One of the other reasons that societies of African continents are diverged and divided into small Kabilas is where they will always have anonymity and discrimination. This is true to some extent, but it is not due to diversity. It is due to quality and extent of diversity. India is diverse country with more than 28,000 casts and sub-casts but as united common value system. These African Nations are led by stability with leaders, so leadership crisis is not reason.

The reason is the **Quality of leadership** and development or upgradation of leadership quality had not taken place to tackle the needs or challenges of generations. The reasons for underdevelopment have been defined for nations as poor governance, corruption, Poor Education and Poor Health care. These are **symptoms, not root causes**. It is a shearing failure of the **Quality of leadership,** which obviously produced around leaders' layer of poor quality, which was in no way connected to and having willpower to solve even the basic needs of people. Society, our communities, our organisation, and we individuals follow the same route.

We easily consider Symptoms for Action, but the Root cause is different. If we are not working on root causes, then our huge resources will be colossal waste.

The complete flow of Process travels the Path to work on Root cause, and Root cause provides the Binding Principle to Leaders as Individuals or as Societies. The clearer Binding Principals will produce the Clear Purpose. For Clarity in Binding principle is/ is not matrix can be useful.

For reference, look at the below table.

Finding Binding Principal for Purpose:

Sl No	Categories	Symptom	Root Cause Specific	Binding principal	Purpose
1	Nation	Poor Governance	Quality of Leaders with **Intent** to drive public welfare Selfless rather than retaining Power	**Intent, Power**	
		Corruption			
		Health care			
		Education			
2	Society	Discrimination	Retain the special status to enjoy the Supremacy	**Special Status, Supremacy**	
		Inequality			
		Crime			
		Conflicts			
3	Organisation	Poor Sales Growth	Quality of Leaders with	**Intent, Value**	

		Tough Competition	Intent to set the Vision of organisation to add Value in employee	**Addition**	
		Unsatisfied Customer			
		Unsatisfied Employee			
4	Individual	Unfulfillment	Taking Responsibility to Change in deep rooted Habit, replacing with Healthy habits	**Responsibility Habit**	
		Lack of Socialization			
		Health Issue			
		Lack of Focus			

Validating your Binding Principal for Purpose:

Sl No	Categories	Binding principal	Is	Is Not	Potential Purpose
1	Nation	**Intent, Power**	Intent of leaders is to serve and uplift the people	Taking undue benefits or Focusing on self is not intent	To Serve the People
			Scientifically Transfer of energy is Power	Not Transferring Energy to the people, you are responsible for	Empower People
2	Society	**Special Status, Supremacy**	Special Status is to Guide and make society Productive	Special status not to capture resources using privileges	Making Society Productive
			Supremacy of Sun to	Supremacy is not to get	Providing equal

			enlighten all without discrimination	thing done out of moral and constitutional ambit	opportunity without Discrimination
3	Organisation	**Intent, Value Addition**	Intent of leaders is to serve and uplift the people	Taking undue benefits or Focusing on self is not intent	To Serve the People
			Value addition is to balancing the personal growth of people synchronized with organisational growth	Value addition is not fulfilling wishes	Value Addition
4	Individual	**Responsibility Habit**	the willingness to accept responsibility is only difference between leader and followers	Responsibility is not about blaming for the incidence of your life	Self-Balancing
			Habit is deep routed automatic process which keep happening without your Notice	Habit is not occasional success	Making & Breaking Habit

Relation between Potential Purpose and Purpose:

Purpose is always beyond only you. Purpose always connects with service and value addition to your customers, Societies, Communities or Organisations. If your activities or Goals are planned only to benefit you, that cannot be purpose. It was Titan's thought that we received from Susamya. We started clapping in between.

Susmya humbly accepted our gratitude and said yet more deeply to understand dearest game changers.

Astrid had a question, Susamya, in reference matrix, you had explained Potential purpose. Are Potential purpose and purpose the same thing?

Susmya applauded, very good question, Dear, indeed, it is not the same. When Potential purpose is refined with better clarity and self-reflections like balancing your interest, Values, strengths and sense of fulfilment it turns into purpose.

Aligning Purpose:

Sports Metaphor:

Most of us shall learn that Metaphors are powerful tools for great leaders. It provides opportunity to put complex things into a simple way.

We have now challenges in our day-to-day life to perform our absolute best, high degree of performance, Vitality, acceptance in Society and many more, but what it takes to achieve, we have never thought of. When we are taking resolution on body building, we precisely take care of input in the form of Food, Gym, etc. When we plan a healthy life, free from stress and anxiety, we recalibrate our lifestyle, and we meditate. In each one of the cases, we put the consciousness on inputs, which make us better.

Now, the same input to get better in profession to which we belong, the life which we dream for ourselves and our families; in the society where we want to build up our credibility, we generally do not pay enough attention to the input required from us. The type of leadership quality is required in us and a gradual development of those qualities from one level to various next levels.

Folks, there is one area which is the best metaphor.

Human for continuous absolute best reason is performance and fitness relation visual to all of us, this function is sports. Just think of lifestyle of high-performer sports stars. They wake up early morning, meditate daily or use some modern focus-enhancing techniques; next step they go for Gym or brisk running and align their food habit with the type of sports they are in. if athletes, they prefer rigid proteins and mindful carbohydrates, or some other sports like football or Hockey player, they prefer Nutrient rich breakfast like Oatmeal Nuts, Fruits and Non-Dairy Milks, then they go for Practice in their respective games. For their Mental toughness, they watch motivating, an extraordinary achievement with willpower such as Videos or powerful audio or the thrilling moments of their game so their mental diet is also aligned. To your surprise, they change according to need, even their bathing habits like taking Ice bath, relaxation bath in which a particular amount of water, like rain will fall in continuity; there will be many variations, like with closed eye condition with music, statue position, etc. They aligned their way of life what there sports demand not what other factors tempt them.

This is Sports metaphor, whatever we want to achieve in the respective area. We had to align completely ourselves considering the demand of our dream. How many of us read the magazine of your industry advancement and best practices? If you are in farming how many in us have continuously enquired about the most demanding crops in the nearest market? Year-wise some improvement methods, the impact analysis with Natural pesticides. **Things which are being done to survive will always produce the result of survival.** Success in life is not for those who run fast, but for those who keep running and are always on the move in the direction of Goal. This Sports metaphor is an amazing technique to align ourselves to the Maximum possible to the profession or stage in which we want to be successful.

It was late evening and end of our first session with Susamya. With the learning of purpose cycle, we had deeply awakened that "Why do we do something?"

We had to meet again in the early morning and we went to get prepared for another exciting day.

2. Fuelling Productivity Cycle:

2nd Session was started next day at 8 AM, after all the morning rituals. Susmya started, Folks, first day, you learnt about the first step of Leadership Quality development. Purpose cycle is indeed very important because you start a deliberate journey of special self-development to turn into leaders like molten metal starts solidifying. Now, we will start second Step Productivity Cycle

Welcome, once again to the Leadership Quality Development session, Susmya lauded with phenomenal energy. We echoed the energy level. Dear champions of growth and knowledge, in this transformative journey, you will unlock your full Leadership potential.

For Fuelling productivity, three things are very important.

- Know your Priorities
- Barricade your Distractions
- Processing Vision to Value

Priority:

Focused Approach Law of 80 -20: Law of 80:20 was initially given by an Italian versatile engineer, Vilfredo Pareto; he discovered in Italy, 80 % of lands belong to 20 % of people. Post this analysis, various functions and sectors like Finance, Agriculture, Management, Human development, and Software development had researched and analysed deeply and found that 80: 20 is a magical combination, here 20 % is the maximum and 80 % minimum. For example, maybe 90% of improvement can be seen with 10% efforts. A few renounced real-life examples are truly instrumental.

- In 2002, Microsoft noted that 20 % of the most reported bugs caused 80% error and crashes.
- US Health Department revealed that 20% of patients use 80 % of health resources.

Swrve, an analytic and app marketing firm, analysed and found that 0.15 mobile gamers use 50 % app Which generated for free.

- World's two largest wine makers and distillers in USA revealed that 10% of drinkers contribute to 50% of consumption.
- According to Hua–Zhong, normal University in China, 20% of sports players from Tennis, fencing snookers, Hockey, volleyball, and baseball, naming a few out of 12 different sports analysed, enjoy 80% success and Prize money.
- As per reports from Economies of the Balkan and the Eastern European Countries, a study on GDPs of all major countries studied between 1980 and 2016, and again forecast extended till 2022 revealed that 20% of the richest countries contribute to 90% of GDPs.

These were a few examples and many consultancies; analysts have tracked and found it widely accepted almost everywhere, and leadership Quality development is not an exception.

- 80 % of revenues of organisations come from 20% of customers
- 20% of productive people contribute 80% of results in organisation.
- 80 % of our time is generally spent with 20% of the closest people in our lives.
- 80% of social media shares are by 20% of posts.
- 80% of time spent on 20% activities.
- 20% of your TV channels are watched 80% of the time.

Now, one thing will be running in your mind, folks, that this Pareto law is very common and what is new in it.

They nodded yes after listening carefully to this magical principal.

Difference is the way we look at this to find the best; it is same as everyone knowing that an apple falls down from the tree, but an observation from Newton gives a different perspective on gravitational theory.

For leadership, it works to utilise efficiency and effectiveness.

- For Leadership, Pareto Principal works to find 20% of strengths which cause 80% of success, hold it close to the chest and keep capitalising on it with precision and effectiveness.

- Identify 20% of weaknesses and 20% habits, which drain your energy and restrict you from being good to great.

- Funnel down the Pareto Principle of second layer for quicker and better results. Even in 20% of 20% will be causing 80% of 80% better results, or in second case, derailing your betterment, so the new equation is - 4% of your strengths cause 64% of results and 4% of your weaknesses cause 64% of your mediocrity. In paper, it looks like so strong like Indian cricket team, all laughed together, but in reality, it requires a focused approach for long term.

Identify all your distractions, including digitals; fill your activity and time with Quality.

How to identify activity and time with Quality, Astrid asked; this is a very unique question, she replied.

This is commonly called Onion method to identify. Onion has multiple layers like human activity and time running multiple things at instance. But each layer in Onion is unique. Make your activity and time unique. Talking to family members and friends and reading messages parallel shows your time and activities are not unique; taking food while watching television shows your process is not unique; preparing reports while attending conference calls are merely physical presence.

Barricade Distraction: Aristotle once said,

"The greatest threat to the state is not faction but distraction."

Loss of productivity due to performing undesirable activities which are in no way supporting your aspiration is called distraction. Nowadays, we are in the era of Distraction. Numerous surveys had thrown the light on Distraction.

You are sitting with your family, engaged in memory of some beautiful moment and parallel messaging to your clients - This is a mild form of distraction. This is an example of not doing the right thing at the time for which it is meant. Distractions are like flowing rivers; you cannot barricade the water, but you can change the root. Distraction can be replaced with awareness and Mindfulness. Let us try to understand food wastage, which is annually estimated at 1.3 billion Tons across the supply chain throughout the world. Many strata across the globe do not get the food; this resource is limited, and we do not have right to waste the food even on our own plates. France government has enforced the law for supermarkets to donate food waste in good condition to Charity or convert it into animal feed or Compost or Energy. Our distraction is a similar waste; we are spending too much time on social media when we can channel this time to reviewing our Kids' studies, helping spouses arrange some events for kids around or helping elderly. Even though it is our personal time, this limited resource cannot be morally right to waste. Unfortunately, each one of us does not have an idea of how much productivity is lost due to distractions we do across the globe. The best way to manage distraction is to first understand what your distraction is, how frequently, in what condition and with which trigger it arrives.

Distraction can be categorized broadly in categories based on today's scenario except baring some rare situations in four categories.

Digital Distraction: This distraction slowly changing into Addiction is the biggest challenge of Today and even seems more challenging into future.

Our life in every way getting connected with the new Gadgets, and each new addition increases the range of Digital distraction. It contains all possible gadgets and electronics mediums from our Mobile laptop, television messaging, Notification, Music player, social media, Online shopping, and Virtual friendship. The most productive time, energy and skill deficiencies are happening today due to compelling misuse. These digital distractions are major cause of lack of focus and concentration, which is a major element of leadership.

Emotional Distraction: Our leadership Quality with Emotional Distraction is like a bird with a broken wing. It will not fulfil the purpose it is meant for. Emotional Distractions examples are grudges in your hearts, past unpleasant memories, Mistakes Humiliation pulling your attention, Relationship issues, feelings of discrimination, Loneliness, and neglected thoughts, which are more to thinking about the problem and consequences of problem rather than solutions.

Imaginary distraction by Mind: If you conquer your imaginary distraction, you will conquer yourself. These Imaginary distractions are all human habits where consequences derived are real, but problems are mostly imaginary or Blind. Imaginary Distractions are Anger, Hate, Blame, shame, Regret, Guilt, Fear, doubt, Jealous, insecurity, frustration and threatened. This distraction is single most significant contributor today to define the culture of a Nation, society, an organisation or an Individual. We cannot hold any leadership quality in our vessel with these tiny productivity vampires.

Multitasking Distraction: Eating toast in the shower is the ultimate multitasking; to do two things at once is to do neither. We all have seen or practised Eating Meals while talking on phone and watching our favourite TV shows; attending Teams meetings while preparing presentations for next meeting, and replying to a WhatsApp message to your business partner. These Practices are result of Broken Focus syndrome.

Multitasking does not mean not performing many activities but not to doing at the same time.

Now, let us understand the science behind this distraction; our Brain is designed to love Pleasure and avoid pain. A study by Princeton University and University of California revealed that our attention switches from maximum focus to taking a scan of surroundings four times every second. This cycle of attention to switch from primary activity to scanning the surroundings is an attempt to search for something more pleasurable. Another study from Harvard University says that 47% of the time people are thinking about something apart from what they are doing. It is Mind wandering. Now, we know that brain has constantly in search of better pleasure, and it also has 47% of time for mind wandering. This both combinedly

are reason for distraction. It produces same chemical called dopamine to brain, which is responsible for addiction.

How to control Distraction? She asked.

Now, this is more important after understanding the distraction. If you can't measure it, you can't manage it.

Measure your digital distraction through awareness; it may not be in minutes, but start roughly in hours.

Number of times social media log in, keep looking for notifications in smart phones, television time, etc. In 2020, average time spent on social media by worldwide internet users was 145 minutes; eMarketer's data published in 2019 says that average time spent by adults in US on Smart phone was 3 hours 45 Minutes a day. A person picks up smart phone ranging from 58 to 113 times in a day without need. These average data will throw the light on controlling overuse of this area.

Minimise social media use and use it constructively. Do not prefer so many social media accounts rather than choose the one which suits your aspirations.

8-8-2-2 Rule: Keep internet off at 8 hours at your workplace; if you need it badly, try to use intermittently; maybe every 2 hours for 5 minutes.

Put your smart phone away and switch off or in-flight mode during your sleep time, including time of sleeping rituals. These 8 hours are magic for your inner peace

Next 2-2 stands for two hours before sleep, which is your family and dinner time will give undivided attention to your loved one. Other 2 hours stand for the morning after waking up. It is required for your health, strength and creativity. This time is for morning rituals, yoga, meditation, workout or morning walk, sports, etc. based on individual choice.

Emotional Distraction and Imaginary Distraction:

Are you required deeper thought and higher effort because it is not as visual as digital distraction?

Countering these Distractions required a shift in the mindset of solution-oriented; you had a fight with your colleagues or your spouse, and now, your distraction is continuing for a week; just think, why? Because you all are thinking about the problem, it happened. Might be, you are right. You all are thinking about the mistakes of your spouse or your colleagues who compelled you to fight. Now, just stop taking the responsibility for the relationship and think about how to resolve it. When you concentrate much on the faults, you shall be at fault. When you always focus on the solutions, you shall always be a solution.

All the imaginary distractions are triggered by incidents; you must attach caution behaviour with this. Note down in your journals and practice it to replace the situation. Like if you are angry, try to have a slight smile; do not express yourself or make a decision for that moment; take water if situation permits, be silent for a moment, focus on breath, be mindful and respond accordingly. **If you are patient in one moment of anger, you will escape a hundred days of sorrow**. Sometimes, these interconnected activities cause distraction. Fear leads to anger, Anger leads to hate, and Hate leads to suffering.

Multitasking Distraction: Multitasking is the most misunderstood activity; Multitasking is fine if you have scheduled two activities at two different times. Distraction is when at the same time you are attempting multiple activities. Prioritising activities will be key to avoid Multitasking Distractions. It will make you more efficient and effective. Have you ever thought about why All Governments have different ministries and why organisations have different functions? Why in our mall's food junction, clothes section, Kids play section, etc. are well layout, because they all wanted to avoid this distraction and make us more organised. So, blaming organisations or situations for multitasking may not lead to a solution. Multitasking creates a dopamine-addiction feedback loop, effectively rewarding the brain for losing focus and constantly searching for external stimulation. Multitasking divides leader's attention and leads to confusion and weakened focus.

Vision to Value processing: Leadership is long-lasting endeavour. We all have by born leadership qualities only at different stages, our leadership levels are different. Then, for aspiring youth of any chronological age, what is the approach to becoming better and take transition to the next level of leadership. Challenges that are created by our current level of effort can't be solved by that same level of effort. Now, we must change the way we work.

We must start adding value to solve these Challenges.

This is the continuity loop of one's productivity cycle.

Interact with different strata of people and experiment with unfamiliar ways to get things done. During initial days of your leadership, your action, your novelty, and your innovation may be very small, but connecting people and resources for the goal, which matters to your society, community and organization will start fuelling your thinking. The same will be noticed by people. Leadership is the capacity to translate vision into Value. Strength of mountains is useless unless it is converted into binding particles. This does not mean we shall leave our Morning ritual, self-improvement activity, and strengthening ourselves. Action and implementation of ideas are complimentary to your self-improvement activity.

Leadership Habits Cycle:
Making and Breaking Habits- Compounding - Consistency

Habits are defined as deeply-routed actions that we all perform with no effort and consciousness; it is mostly driven by subconscious mind. Habit is the single most contributing constituent which defines leaders. Great leaders are not great because of what they achieved and what potential they have in the people. They can achieve and build potential because they have installed the all-good habits which work for them. Today, we are in a time of machines and automation. It is meant to reduce Human effort, and physical challenges, and every time, it produces same good results; we can see the benefit of lifts in multistage buildings and electronic machines. The mechanisms first install them to work, and maintenance is based on frequency or requirements. Human Habits work in the same way. It is effortless when it is installed; it ensures same result every time and works like a system in you. Habit is the built-in automation within living creatures. The best part is all temporary distractions work in conscious mind, and subconscious mind works effectively even in adverse times. What the desired benefit must extract out of subconscious mind is to install it for betterment, and recalibrate time to time to be a more productive automatised leader.

Our Habit functions outside of the awareness. A different study reveals that 40% of our daily activities are habitual. If these 40% habits are aligned to support our aspiration, then productivity will be multiple times. One article published in Harvard Business Review says that 95% of our behaviours are habitual, and only 5% we consciously act. Forming habits initially may have individual root causes, but how habits continue is for sure discovered. It is the Trigger of events, place, incidents, and timing. For example, smokers have different triggers to smoke with Alcohol or coffee or a particular shop, before rushing to rest room. Similarly, habits of waking up early, Morning exercise, and brushing your teeth in morning are time-triggered.

Idea is here to monitor your habits carefully for a few days and continue the habits which are supportive of your Dream and Mission, replacing the habits which are a hurdle in your leadership Quality.

Science behind Habits:

You are fully tired in a day standing in your organic garden farm; it is your lunch time, and how pleasant you feel in the mild breeze beneath the tree. Our Brain is one that is constantly looking for pleasure, something better and rewarding itself with activity. Similarly, it has another feature where brain continuously looks to save efforts which give it rest like a tired farmer and focus on its primary activity to keep looking for something more pleasurable. During this process, brain makes any routine into habits. It is a three-step process that starts with Reminder, Routine and Reward.

Reminder: The trigger that cues your action or behaviour. Routine: the action or behaviour itself. Reward: the sense of fulfilment or benefit that you get from doing an action or by following behaviour.

Let us understand this scenario.

Reminders: This type of trigger tells your brain to go into "automatic mode" and perform a specific behaviour. Such as, if you have to drink more water during the working day, seeing a water bottle on your desk or work Place is a reminder to drink up, which has substantially changed during weekend of taking

Water because you are at home and there is no Reminder.

Routines Here is the Actual Process of behaviour. To continue with the example about drinking water from that bottle at Work place is the routine.

Rewards This is the last step of this process, which closes the loop. Rewards help to continue the behaviour (routine) and create a new habit. In case of the water example, the reward for drinking water is quenching thirst, preventing dehydration and maintaining Energy levels.

Since 40% of our daily activities are habitual, it is important to have happy Habits, Healthy Habits, Positivity Habits, Social Connectivity Habits and productivity Habits. If you are already filled with these habits, continue with them and work on the effectiveness of habits, but if you have Non-healthy and Unproductive habits, then these habits have to be broken, and new habits need to be installed. This Process is called Breaking Habits and Making Habits.

For Making and Breaking habits, Repetition is key to succeed, and there is defined timeline. Have you ever thought why so many wellness, Business, and Sports programmes are called for 21 days challenges, 28 Days Challenges, or 30 Days Challenges....? Actually, this is an attempt to form a habit. Thanks to University College, London, whose study on 96 students based on daily behaviour and converting them into Habits are deeply studied and concluded.

Habit formation takes as per Difficulty of Activities to individual variation from 21 days to as long as 254 days. If a glass of water after lunch is to be installed as habit, it will take only 21 days. Now, here comes the direct reply of on average activities and on average individuals. **Habit Formation takes 66 Days** exactly. This must be repeated for 66 days and shall not be Consecutive 3-day gap.

Breaking Habit and Making Habit: The chains of habit are too weak to be felt until they are too strong to be broken.

Breaking Habits will start by Listing Down those all-unproductive activities that either impact your health, waste your time, or look socially awkward, like consuming alcohol, Smoking or consuming too much coffee, watching TV, continuously checking email, WhatsApp Notification, biting fingernails, Not bathing every day and lists are countless.

Step 1: Give the thought why you want to replace them and what benefits you will get after replacing this habit. Focus continuously on the benefits, like quitting Alcohol will reduce the frequent clash with your spouse; bathing every day will keep you feeling fresh and in good odoriferous.

Step 2: Always start with easy-to-replace habits because replacing Habits is also a Habit. Your pleasure-loving brain will oppose replacing tough habits.

Step 03: To Break Habit, Attack the Reminder process and replace the trigger. Willpower alone to quit will not work during breaking habit, like if watching television during dinner is habit to break, change the dining place which is not accessible to TV during dinner. After dinner, reminder is to go for smoke, and then have a walk with kids and spouse. Replace your freezer from beer to health drink.

Step 04: For Making a Habit, be very specific about why you want to form a positive habit; think about a long-term vision, like morning Yoga, workout and Meditation, which will keep your healthy life long, and reading habit of books will keep your perspective clear in turbulent times. Socialising and helping communities instead of watching Netflix will enrich your network.

Step 05: Reverse Trigger is something like concept of Reverse swing in cricket where a Baller swings the used ball as similar to a new ball. Here, make a list of old triggers and how to fit them into New Trigger for making a positive habit. For Example, when you wake up in morning, the first thing is now common to check social media notifications on your mobile. We keep Mobile mostly beside. To changetriggers, place your mobile out of your bedroom. Place some powerful books beside you, and Journaling stuff nearby to start your day with creativity.

Step 06: Accomplishment with Reward System: Habits keep going because of reward system. You have a trigger to sleep after morning breakfast. After waking up, you will feel lousy yet satisfied because of reward. These are the similar reasons why after watching hours of news, you will feel satisfied. Another way, if your Plan is writing a journal after breakfast, you must feel it and feel the accomplishment may not be natural in the beginning, but certainly after few repetitions.

Compounding and Consistency:

Albert Einstein said - Compounding is the eighth wonder of the world; this compounding is not only for wealth, this is equally true for your Health, Leadership Development, Relationships and everything where very small but consistent investments of yours bring cheer to you and your surrounding.

If you pick a Single Coin and double it the next day and repeat this for 30 days, it will be Rs. 53 68 709 12/-.

The world record of Folding A4 Size paper in half is with Britney Gallivan, who did it 12 times. Earlier, it was considered very challenging more than 7 Times. Let us look at the impact of compounding.

If A4 size paper in half can be done in 30-Fold, it will take you in space nearly 100 Km.

42 folds will make us reach Moon.

Now think, if we are honing our Skills a little yet significantly every day, utilising our time and focus every day consistently, it will give the same impact like compounding.

If your focus improves everyday 0.01 %, after 12 months, your focus will increase by 3.7 times.

The compounding effect is the operating system that has been running your life. There will be good years, and there will be bad years, but the compounding will continue unabated, so for compounding and consistency, develop three skills.

Discipline: Discipline is a key tool to develop consistency in behaviour cycle. People with Discipline are architects of their own beliefs and actions. They will not fall into materialistic comparison, Temptation and Discrimination.

Disciplined people will always align with the values that they have in outer world and what they are from within. Practice being as original as you are without hurting and passing judgement on situations and people.

Work Breakdown: Work breakdown is a tool to automatise the beginning stage of making habits and putting it into path of compounding. A challenging skill, an entirely new learning you want to develop, then set a time with a trigger for 2 hours daily, for next 66 days. Once it is turned into habit, continue with intention of continuous improvement.

Time frame: Every highly successful story you hear fails to mention the years spent preparing for the overnight success: The sports player who practiced every day, the business owner who worked on their idea for years, or the Mutual fund managers who spent their weekends looking for balance sheets and analysis. These all are results produced with compounding. Compounding takes time, and we have to develop the discipline against conventional mindset to get the quickest win. A quick win will be hard to maintain genuinely. This is our consumer behaviour, which turns into an advertisement to cut fats by 60% within a week. Get rid of neck and back pain in seven days like stuff.

Self-Balancing Cycle:

Wellness balance - Finance balance - Personal life

Wellness balance Universal Rule of Leadership:

In this World, all the products, Services and activities, which are happening in legal and moral ambit made for wellbeing of humans. Either we manufacture a needle or a plane, or we service an online portal or a coffee stall, or it is an NGO or newspaper delivery boy, the one common thing is that they all are made to make human life better. In other words, they contribute to our Quality of life. Here, one thing on leaders shall be clear that leaders in actual do not take care of businesses; they take care of People who take care of the businesses; same is true in case of social leaders, Team captains or at the minute level, everyone. So, the Universal law takes shape here that "First virtue of any leader is to contribute in betterment of Quality of life of all with whom they are involved." This is not only good for organization, Societies and communities, but this is good for cycle. A better understanding of this cycle proportionately will produce a better leader.

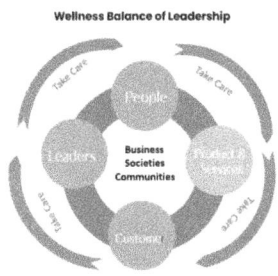

Quality of life can be understood as all the fundamental needs of Humans which include Physical, Mental and Social wellness of self and family with the space of Values, personal expectations, and Goals of life. So, everything else is ensured if leaders take care of people. This is the pillar of wellness. Take charge of your ecosystem to create a wellness balance which will self-balance individuals, societies and communities around you. **Product of Taking care of people and ecosystem around you is leadership quality.**

Personal Life Balance: Element of Personal life is ambience of self, your family and friends. The ambience of self shall be first step to boosting yourself which will further strengthen your interaction with Family and Friend and surround you with super balance.

Health is a Priority -Prioritise your Physical and Mental health. Your Diet upgrade shall continue for Physical, and the most importantly, Mental Diets like meditation, Learning and practicing gratefulness, and Mental interaction of Great thoughts, which eventually change the universe.

Practise your Vibes: Three things are common in all great achievers, they are Early-Riser, Good Readers and the Most important but always ignored, Source of Energy level. The energy of mind is the essence of life. Watch carefully about your energy level when you interact with someone; when you perform the action, this energy creates your Aura, frequency and Vibration. For creating this vibe of energy, pamper yourself as a priority. Wear Good clothes, smell good, the way you walk, the way you talk with complete eye contact and with absolute enthusiasm, carefully selecting positive words, etc. This is the raw material for your Leadership Quality development.

Family and Friends Matter: Do not take love and association for granted from your family and friends. To build the tribes of nears and Dears needs enormous effort, time, caring and respect for them. Your Great performance as a leader is your deep relationship with your work. Your personal life balance is your deeper relationship with your family and friends. Nothing grows well without space and air; the same is true for your relationship; give the space with your time, emotions, undivided attention, respect and appreciation. Help them in need, celebrate your great moments with them and the Trust foundational principle that holds all relationships.

Finance Balance:

"If we command our wealth, we shall be rich and free. If our wealth commands us, we are poor indeed" - Edmund Burke.

Financial freedom contains two elements: One is continuously upgrading the Earning based on ethics and value; second and the most important is the habit of saving. The habit of financial saving is itself an education; it fosters every virtue, teaches self-denial, cultivates a sense of order, trains forethought, and so broadens the mind. Here, Financial Balance is not about being Rich but more about to forecasting even with some unforeseen incidents in your life to avoid the trouble of basic needs of self and family.

Personal Finance is more about personal than finance; we see people earning millions but encountering financial trouble and a person earning relatively less but managing finances very well. Reason behind this is to define the requirement and use purposefully. An article recently published in 2021 -September reveals that an American spends at least 18000 dollars per year on non-essential like throwing leftovers or expired foods, buying overpriced beverages, and impulsive buying, name a few. Finance balance will strengthen you in times of adversity.

Good Finance Balance: Three elements of your Finance, Must, Want, and savings must be balanced. The Golden Number of balance points is 50-30-20 rule. You have to earn a minimum where 50% of your earnings can take care of must-items like basic needs. 30% of your earnings can accommodate your wants / Fun and emotional spending.

20% of your earning must be saved and shall go into compounding Investment.

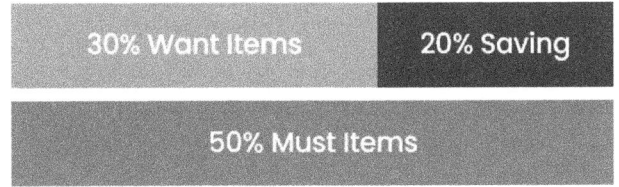

Golden Tolerance Limits: for Must or Essentials:

Under 20%: Compromised Future aspects

Under 35%: in Safety Zone

35–50%: in Balance

50–65%: in Danger Zone

More than 65%: in Crash Zone

Golden Tolerance Limits: for wants, Fun and emotional spend:

More than 30%: Spend extravagantly

20-30%: Wants in Balance

Less than 20%: All Work and No Play may lead Health Issues

Golden Tolerance Limits: for saving

0-5%: Inconsistent Saver

6-12%: Solid Saver

12-20%: Strong Saver

20% +: Super Big Saver

50% +: Essentials and Want compromised may lead Concerns

This personal Finance management is like a brick on which structure is made; if you are not a natural finance manager from your personal life, then you are acting as managing finance in organizations, societies and communities.

Every compulsion put upon yourself as leaders to act polite, obedient, and balanced creates a difference between genuinely you and your Act. Difference between genuinely you and your Act = **Imbalance**

Managing these imbalances completes balancing cycle:

SUMMING IT UP:
- Leadership Quality Development is 4th step of the Leadership Development Process.

➢ This step focuses on the Core Quality of leadership that will be visible in handling day-to-day Challenges.

➢ The purpose of Leadership Quality Development is to strengthen the fort of the soul to stay strong in all the storms of life.

➢ Purpose cycle, Productivity cycle, Habit cycle and Balancing cycle are four steps for activating Leadership Quality.

➢ Purpose cycle has three depths called sub-steps to execute. Find the purpose, **Validate the purpose** with substantial data/observation and Align your activities around purpose.

➢ Productivity cycle similarly has, Priority setting, Barricading distraction and Vision to value creation.

➢ Habit cycles have sub-steps, Making and Breaking habits, compounding and consistency.

➢ Balancing cycle has wellness, personal and Personal finance.

CHECK YOUR UNDERSTANDING:

➢ What are the key Qualities of leadership you would like to develop to tackle challenges Effectively?

➢ What is the importance of Purpose cycle? Write a few more examples of metaphor of alignment like Sportsmen?

Right down your top 15 priorities in life, funnel down only the top 3 has to complete, and observe the method of selection carefully.

➢ Write down all your distractions, categorise them as per book and make an elimination plan.

➢ Write all your habits; what are habits to be broken and replaced with good habits?

➢ Write a detailed for framework Wellness, personal and personal finance.

Chapter - 05

Leadership System Thinking

We all were excited for our next journey. It would be life-changing as the last word of Susamya. The 15-hour journey from Chennai to Zurich was truly orchestral with Qatar Airways. The best part of Qatar Airways was the nature in everything. Food to the way crew members attend you. It was a happy landing in Zurich on Saturday in the early morning at 6 AM. It was love at first sight with tidy, artful, cultivated and sweeter Zurich. As we entered the main Lawn of Zurich airport, a person greeted us with a confident smile, Hello Amrit, Astrid and John. Ooh, how do you know? Astrid asked. The man in perfect sense of humility replied, I saw your photos in Dr. Hudson's farm house, my Tribe.

I belong to same club of leaders. He continued, as per Dr. Hudson's request, all your arrangements are scheduled, handing over key for self-drive Skoda Octavia. We entered into the car. Each seat has a golden colour's Schedule menu. Astrid read the headings, taking charge of driving seat.

"The most evolved leaders put their heart, mind, intellect, and soul to turn into Systemic leaders"

A beautiful quote, Astrid said, and we nodded in Yes.

Follow the instructions to meet your Mentor:

Dr. Hudson farmhouse

Horgen

We put the address on map and started the journey. Horgen is outskirt of Zurich, having a fabulous combination of forest, agriculture small industries and residential. We arrived at our destination, which was a truly nature's home. Hudson Farm house was on the bank of Zurich Lake. We are received by a person fairly Tall with a magical spark in his eye, and legs full of dust and bare. He hugged warmly and said, welcome to Zurich, my tribes. I am glad to be host of the people from the land where the guest is God. It was a proud moment for Amrit and John to hear about India.

We stayed in the guest house, had a rest, and as suggested by Dr. Hudson, we planned to meet at 3 PM.

We met at 3 PM, and Dr. Hudson took us on tour of Farm house. It had four parts; one part had fruits, mostly apple trees, second part had herbs, third part were vegetables and the last part had some commercial Agri products related to cooking Oil, like walnuts, Sunflower and Linseed. It is a super excited walk, Dr. Hudson, John broke the silence. Yes, dearest

John, this ecosystem is my life. I built this with my best courage to move one step ahead of Fear. Ooh, Really, Astrid asked.

Yes, Astrid, in the recession of 1990-1993 in Switzerland, I had stiff pressure in my global agriculture research company. Staffs were slashed by 33%; working time was up by 40%. We had no time on weekdays, even for essentials. Losing some of my good colleagues, high working hours, and health issues had started a continuous spark in my brain, but my purpose was not clear. One day, I realised my responsibility was compelled by an incident of food poisoning. I broke into regret. One of my close friends suggested visiting Varanasi and meeting Sri Swami. I followed after resigning and completing my contract period with company -this decision was life-changing. I worked with a global organization in top management; I could only understand till then to make a strategy to develop a business, and get revenue in all open markets of the world. Respect the culture to run the business smoothly, contribute to social responsibility to respect the law of land. After travelling to India, I got a new perspective, and new way of thinking. Dr. Hudson had full conviction, spark and energy, continuing the Explanation. I understood that we all are interconnected and interdependent more than a business and revenue. **The Earth is family,** is a Unique selling proposition from India to rest of the world. This way of thinking is revolutionary in solving the problems of today's world. Without such thinking, leadership development is incomplete. Without this thinking, leadership is like a Bulb without a power source.

Astrid was excited to hear more about the practice of thinking; Dr Hudson was explaining, so she asked, what is the name of this thinking process? How does it work?

Dr Hudson Smiled and said, This was the exact purpose, Sri Swami had sent you all here, folks.

This Process of Thinking is Called **System Thinking**. We tried to intervene, but he continued.

A common mistake we commit not to stopping our excitement to hear someone fully; this was perfect time to take this learning.

Dr Hudson further stated System thinking has two facets: One is the structure underlying, which means various components of system, and second is how they are connected to each other.

Never thought like this, Astrid replied. Yes, Astrid, we will start our session from Sunday 7 AM.

System Thinking:

It was a sunny morning with energetic breeze of fresh air in Dr. Hudson's farm house. We met at 7 AM. We all were super excited about the tool of problem-solving in the 21st century - **System Thinking**. Dr. Hudson arrived at the right time; we had a warm hug, had a sip of coffee and started the session.

Good morning, Folks, this is a very important day for the leaders who get introduced to **System Thinking**. Try to understand fully and start practicing. We all this time listened to it in deep silence. Dr. Hudson said, we all are surrounded by a system, made of a system and being influenced by the system. If we consider our life as system, it has many dimensions, naming few -

• Health	• belief	• Office
• Family	• Faith	• Governance
• Friends	• Life style	• Decisions
• Education	• Exercise	• Value set
• Circumstances	• Food	• Money

In this system, there is an inter-relationship between these components and to some degree, they impact our lives. When we see the good or bad in our life, we must try to understand whether things are right or wrong to make your life better every day.

Amrit had a question: Does it mean, once we know that what works and what does not for life, we can give the solution readymade?

Dr. Hudson Smiled and clarified with calm: Amrit, your question has hit the bull's eye. This is how most coaches and solution providers fail. In System thinking, over period of time, we will understand which are generic systems and which are highly specific systems. Life is a highly specific system, which has to be discovered by individual in their own way. Here, the learning is that we must understand the dimensions of life through system thinking, and we must find the relationship and betterment opportunities in life. System thinking is next generation's solution provider tool, and there is a lot more to discover. Only continuous practice can transform us.

Astrid asked a question: Can we find a subsystem in side system?

Of course, Astrid, system can be larger; within system can be subsystems. Within life system, take one example of Health system. Health can be Physical, mental and social wellbeing. Within Physical, it can be Human Body system; within Human body system, we have organ systems, like respiratory system, digestive system, nervous system, endocrine system, etc.

This is mind-blowing, but will it not be too complex to use in real-life solutions? Astrid asked.

The answer of Dr. Hudson was a masterpiece to differentiate novice vs. expert in the function. Dr. Hudson replied with confidence, - System thinking is not only Scientific and not merely mathematics. It is all about experience and Application. If you think about theoretical parts, everything will be complex; only use it for application and derive the scientific result.

Our brain is the most complex system in the known universe. Brain consists of 100 billion nerve cells. The front part of the brain has more than 10 billion neurons. Every single neuron can have up to 100,000 inputs. The front part of the brain itself has one million billion connections. If you count one in every second, it will take 32 million years.

These data on brain are fine, but doctors who operate brain or Brain performance coaches only see the pattern and do not go into the complexity of numbers.

Perfect example, but if it is so practical and gives results, then why is it not popular? I know this question would be hunting, Dr. Hudson said, smiling.

Folks, we know that every day, we use system thinking, but we have not standardised and horizontally deployed the solutions.

When I was in India, I saw a popular game, Cricket. Out of 11 players, the best-suited team was with batter, baller, all-rounder and wicketkeeper. How the most suitable millions of players will be playing in the National team is based on some defined pattern. This is complete system thinking. We cook every day in kitchen, using vegetables, spices, salt, water, and the result is our tasty food. Here, we do not research each ingredient; we only know basic properties of each ingredient.

Today's session was on end, based on our plan to visit Oerlikon Zurich, the vegetable market of all the farmers, who directly sell to households. This

was an extended session to understand System thinking. Next sessions were going to be far more important.

Dr. Hudson's entry was perfect at 7:30 AM. After a tasty yet super energetic breakfast, we started the session.

The session will be in four parts:

- Success story of system thinking
- Close loop Philosophy
- Bricks of system Thinkers
- Brain Storming session

Success story of system thinking:

Success is Walking from Failure to Failure with no loss of enthusiasm - Winston Churchill

Dr. Hudson asked a question.

Do you know why, in almost all cultures, storytelling is powerful tool of learning?

Astrid Replied, because it connects easily.

That is true, Astrid, but meaning is far deeper.

Storytelling promotes system thinking. You have a definite start and end. You cannot disrupt the flow or skip one part of any meaningful story.

This was another eye-opening thought from Dr. Hudson. You saw the type of gratitude and respect being paid by farmers in Oerlikon. This is the outcome of my honest, selfless effort; now, it has become the source of energy to transform millions.

I was part of the management team in a multinational Agri Research and Marketing Agency. Our budget was more inclined towards marketing than research. We were even paying attention to research based on commercial market rather than food-enriched nutrients at affordable prices around the globe. Financial Numbers were important for company rather than transforming agriculture market. The expert Buyers team bought the foods, fruits, and flowers at throw-away prices, and after packaging them in the compelling way, the company was selling at high prices. The situation of farmers and farm workers were not good in and around Zurich. The heavy use of fertilizers was started by farmers due to obvious reasons to increase productivity. Land and water started contaminating. Traditional Agri products which were rich in nutrients were no more in farm. People started to get into health issues. Immunity considerably dropped. Medical business became as important as food.

It is not the case that the Federal government was not taking steps to curb such practice, but in system thinking, breaking the chain is more important than working on the trivial reasons.

John F Kennedy once said -Our problems are man-made; therefore, they may be solved by man, and man can be as big as he wants. No problem of human destiny is beyond human beings.

This was what happened on a fine Friday when I seriously got food poisoning and was admitted to one of the best hospitals in global healthcare

University Hospital of Zurich. Doctors found the reason of Rosti quality which I had for dinner.

What is Rosti, Dr Hudson? Amrit asked gracefully.

Rosti is prepared from grated fried potato with stuffing of cheese, apple and onion; it is part of today's menu.

I found the reason to seek a street vendor near my street where I had Rosti. It was the day I discovered the biggest lesson of my life.

Before I approached, the street vendor rang the bell.

He cried in front of me, based on your recommendation, I bought potatoes, apples, and onions from your farm house, but the quality was poor because too much pesticide was used. Many of my loyal customers had health issues, but I always see them smiling and fit after my food. Now, I am worried about my credibility and losing customers.

John asked a question: You were running this farm house on those days also, was it not?

Dr Hudson Replied: No, John, this farm house I rented as contract farming; this land belongs to my ancestors. I broke from inside; the land from which contaminated grains originated was mine.

Many people who had health issue because of me.

I never met them but indirectly harmed. I felt completely responsible for the Health issues.

No individual raindrop ever considers itself responsible for the flood, but system thinkers are different:

It is easy to dodge our responsibilities, but we cannot dodge the consequences of dodging our responsibilities. I decided to find a solution.

Next morning, I resigned and successfully completed the contract period. Post visit to Varanasi, I made this garden my permanent place. I had known a few farmers who never compromised the quality and natural farming, even in the chaotic period. I made them part of my mission; I am a leader in this field because I am a follower of my mission.

We all in tribe had a clear affirmation: We all connected with an idea with the purest intention where everyone is a leader and Hero of this Mission. We have shared interests, and our way of communication must be we centric than I centric. We love the limitation of self and each other's. Our shared purpose and mission are bigger than individual free will.

It is hard work, perseverance, learning, studying, and sacrifices that established this eco system. Remember this important skill from system thinking that leaders work for society, tribes, Nations, Communities and organisations. Leaders know that success of individual is only instantaneous, and if we want to build to last, then involvement must be larger on win-win. We approached people; we gathered the data from hospitals to track our progress. We focused on wellbeing of people rather than making money. We produced consistently Quality grains organically. People got the option to choose health as an option. Even for the sales manager, the first target in system shall be to provide options to choose the best-suited rather than money-making short cut.

Close loop Philosophy:

Folks, the idea I am sharing is worth understanding deeply and implementing in your life.

All improvements, changes, solutions and progress resemble the tendency to reverse to close the loop. This is a universal philosophy in systems. Let us understand in the diagram, we have a generic problem and are trying to provide

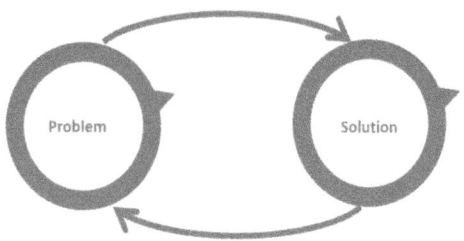

a Solution; then as per close loop philosophy, this problem will most likely have the tendency to repeat. So, the solution does not work due to the lack of System thinking approach. The solution needs support for sustenance. This support of sustenance is called process, systems or rituals. They mean similar. This is the biggest reason that lifestyle diseases are becoming incurable. We are not providing the process of healthy food, sleeping rituals, stress management and regular exercises, but relying on medication. Hence, lifestyle diseases have a tendency to get back to problem once the efficiency of solutions drops.

Irrespective of scientific reason, any quick solution and linear solution must be tested on the impact of closing the loop effect.

This is an amazing concept Dr. Hudson, John backed. Can you throw some more practical examples of close-loop philosophy?

Dr. Hudson said, this is the universal law, just to learn the application and practice.

But I will explain a complete cycle of relationship issues either with your friends, colleagues, partner or relatives. If you are patching up a bad relationship

Around which all the ingredients available which pull down relationship then potentially

Close loop philosophy activates. This is why

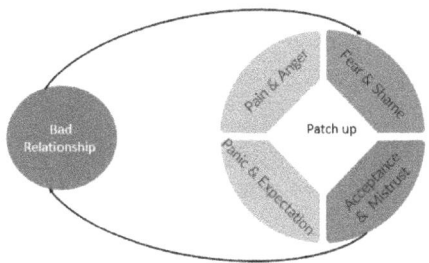

you get time and again conflict in your relationships with colleagues, spouse, friends and Business partners.

System thinking supports you to work not on patch up but rather on ingredients, like Anger, Fear, Mistrust and Expectation, to come out of a bad relationship and nullify the bad impact of a closed loop system.

Now, for coming out of a bad relationship, do not make a quick fix; understand the potential triggers.

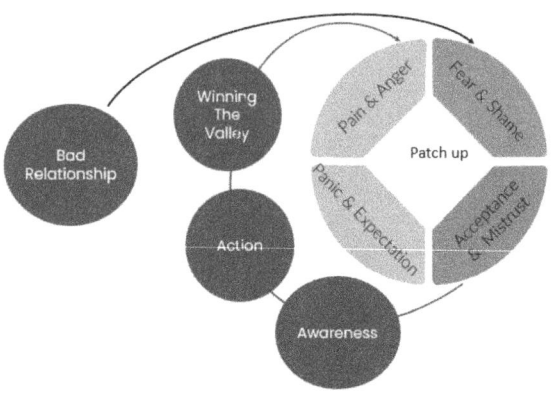

Create awareness of yourself. It is not important who the cause is. It is important as a leader that you take complete responsibility for your relationships.

Start working on this; first, show the sign of improvement through an action. Win on the subject ground, which pulls your relationship down and then go for patch-up. The benefit of this process or system is your problem out of a closed loop. Hope you all got this important leadership skill of using system thinking in relationship management.

Bricks of System Thinker: Now, the next level of challenge we have is "How to develop System Thinkers".

Yup, exactly, Dr. Hudson, Our Mission is to create millions of leaders in all sections of societies, Astrid said.

Dr. Hudson continued - this is not an action but a process. the most prominent bricks for upgrading the individuals into system thinkers.

Process and System oriented:

It means to understand your surroundings deeply and follow the written rules. Being process-oriented makes the possibility for continuous improvement because you know input and output are happening within you and around you. System-oriented keeps you updated.

Once you are aware of yourself and your surroundings, you will be able to connect the dots or interconnectedness of activities better.

Big picture thought process:

Always practice to think about the bigger part of the trend. Generally, we get settled in comfort, but discomfort makes us strong for future, the big picture of thinking.

"First mover Advantage doesn't go to the company that starts up; it goes to the company that scales up." - Reid Hoffman.

Having an idea and looking at the big picture of the idea are two different things. Mr. Jeff Bezos saw the bigger picture of internet shopping in 1994; Tata Sons dreamt of the upcoming software industry in 1968 in India.

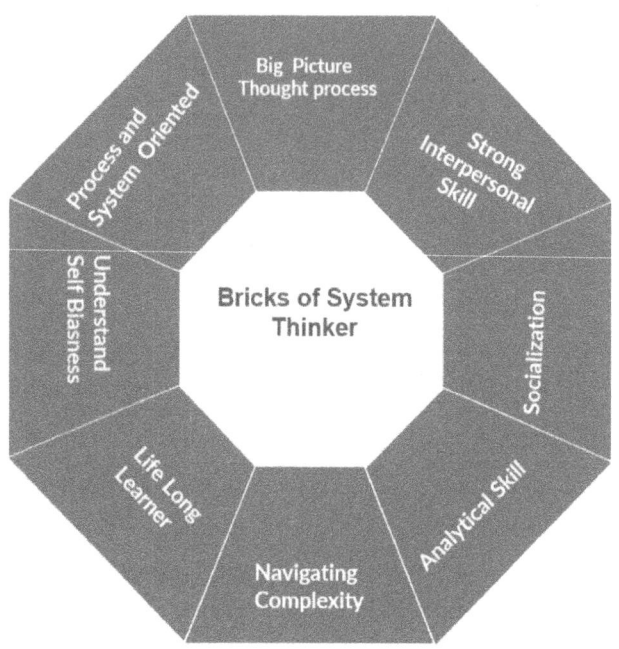

Strong interpersonal skill:

Two types of flow define humans; inside the body, the blood and outside the reflection of Interpersonal behaviour. Interpersonal skill is an art, not a science. The best part of the art is that we learn on the job. Our interpersonal skills are the way we interact, communicate, collaborate and affirm with etiquette. The stronger the interpersonal skill you gain, the better the probability of being a system thinker. When we interact with people, we know the different perspectives, information, success stories and learnings. When you collaborate with people, you learn to approach challenges. All these will help you understand interconnectedness, which is basically system thinking.

Astrid asked a question, Mr. Hudson, what is the one interpersonal skill that is most important?

Dr Hudson replied with grace -Astrid, listening is the most important skill for two strong reasons.

- People always consider listening as an easy skill because of perceptions that Speakers are leaders. Listening develops learning habits in you, and most importantly, empathy and respecting others. Demand vs. Supply rule is applicable even in case of Listening vs. Speaking. Without demand, if you are supplying goods in the market, it may not generate the right revenue. Without listening, if you have a habit of speaking, it may not earn professional and personal dividends.

Wonderful, I never thought like this, John replied.

- When you are truly listening, you are imbibing another's perspective and understanding his or her concern. Now, helping someone's concern, suggesting concern, and understanding her perspective will bring better relationships, which is the first step of influencing people.

This is an even stronger reason, Astrid replied happily.

Socialization: To understand socialization, let us ask a few questions.

- Why does the New Year celebration at Times Square New York energise the complete USA?
- How does the Yoga Day celebration vibrate across globe on 21st June?
- Why is meeting more common in offices?
- Why do we celebrate all the happy moments with family and friends?
- Why do night crawlers enjoy night clubs in groups?
- Why do multi-storey buildings with gated communities become so popular?

The answer to all these questions is same.

To banking upon socialization. Socialization brings openness and information from various perspectives. This information and perspective help people think in system. That is how communities and societies developed appetites against challenges in olden days. There were no formal universities for architects, but the Pyramids and great temples of India were made of collective social information. Indirect support to system thinking through socialization is connected to making humans healthier, happier and more productive. This was outcome of a Harvard study of adult development implemented on 724 men in 79 years.

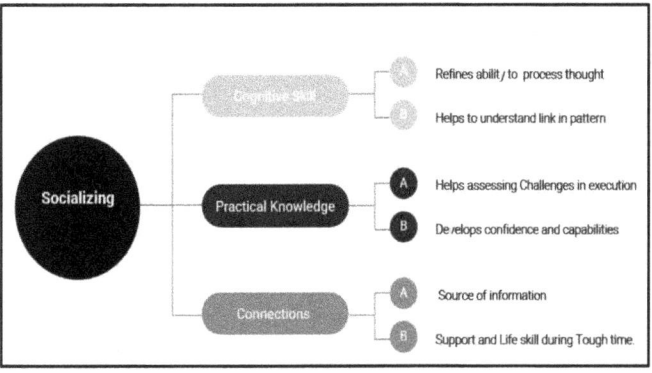

Analytical Thought process: The meaning of analytical thought process is simplifying complex. The link between analytical thought process and system thinkers' strengths goes hand in hand. Analytical thought process considers the nature of interaction, and system thinking considers the impacts of interaction.

Developing system thinking strength is a long-term process, but it reduces a lot more analytical analysis once developed in true sense. Titanic was a classic example where among all superior material and analytical thought processes, many researchers concluded either substandard Rivets, considering them not important, or partially developed standards for rivets could cause the system to be non-functional.

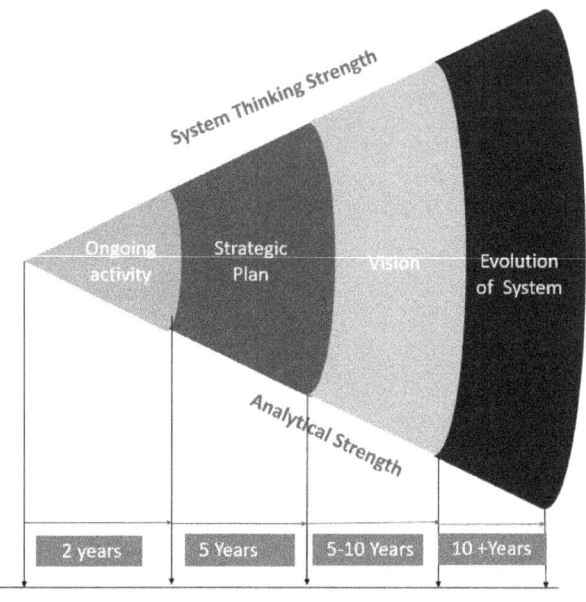

System thinking and Analytical skills do not differentiate if you just think on a day-to-day. If you are thinking two years ahead, system thinking requires more than analytical due to complex conditions unseen. For thinking 5 Years ahead-strategic planning -System thinking starts dominating and continues to dominate if you have a vision for 10 years and beyond.

Navigating complexity: The modern time challenges are as deep everywhere as maritime travellers of olden days. When you are a leader, you have responsibility on your shoulders for people left to you and right to you. Franklin D. Roosevelt's quote, "A smooth sea never made a skilled sailor," the deeper meaning is you must know how to navigate in complex situations like rough sea. Studies on many complex situations suggest three things are most important for navigating complexity.

- **Cut on the fats:** You must give up your few privileges and maybe sometimes even a basic need. A non-value-added activity like your heavy fat must be cut down to prepare against navigating a complex situation.

- **Courage to face with cause:** World War II was one of the complex situations in 20th century. There is one famous saying among diplomats: Russian blood, American money and Churchill's strategy were major factors in the win. All the three cut on the fats had been performed with courage and the respective nation's cause. Russians had a cause to protect motherland, USA wanted to emerge as an economic superpower and Churchill had challenges to protect the life of British spread across the globe as colonial administrators.

- **Away from self-interest:** In the same World War II, Wilhelmina from Netherlands was another popular figure for resistance against German forces. She was in exile, but she involved Dutch people in resistance, her ground understanding and decision-making to give up some lesser important conflicts with Britain for a larger cause made her extremely popular. She could connect to people because of being away from self-interest.

Amrit had a clarification, this is perfect, Dr. Hudson, but for leadership, it would be the most important and challenging to keep going in a complex situation; what are the factors to be considered?

Wow, perfect question, Amrit. Perhaps I could have missed it. This is simple but needs focus to stop it from turning into complex. Build the habit of real-time learning, take feedback on each small step you take, assess carefully, learn from it and keep going. The second step is to keep your eye and ear open; a few things you see but may not be right unless you assess noise around you in a complex situation. It is true vice versa.

Lifelong learners: The road of learning is always under construction. Learning is not only knowledge taking in new things, but it must be taking on new things. There are three ways of learning and their impact on individuals

Shown. The foundation of all learning is definitely from our environment, family and friends; this keeps getting strength lifelong, but direct contribution of shaping you as a system thinker is not so great. Formal education may increase your knowledge, but learning from formal education also does not contribute much to shaping you as system thinker. The biggest contributing factor is lifelong learners, either through self-education, laser-sharp observing, or imbibing experimentation, can add multi-fold System thinking strength.

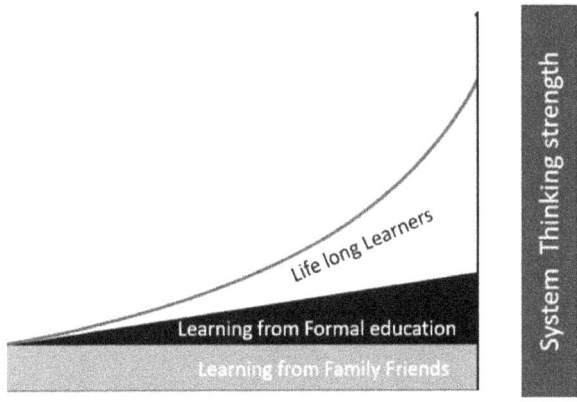

Understand self-bias:

The eye sees only what the mind is prepared to comprehend:

Robertson Davies

As humans, we listen and take forward information that confirms our existing beliefs. Leaders are no exception to this human tendency. Biases are blind spots for system thinkers. As a leader, you must start getting aware of your biases. It is difficult because sometimes this may emerge from your belief system. To get rid of such biases, you must be data-centric, taking holistic feedback and different perspectives. Socializing with large group of people, especially respecting people who have different views may help you create awareness of your biasness. This is the prime reason that classification of different ministries against different portfolios had been created in democracies. Organisation is continuing with different functions with fair autonomy. Biases are real science of people, yet there is a lot more to be discovered, and perhaps, still the best source of input is Indian Santana cultural books.

But here, we are focusing on systematic patterns from truth in decision making, which are basically Cognitive biases. System thinking and leadership are the most impacted by cognitive biases. Examples of cognitive biases are, **judging a situation** based on resemblance of a similar situation, **refusing to think of an** alternative solution for betterment, **giving an opinion/conclusion** which is more socially acceptable rather than bitter truth, **avoiding negative** situation without taking action, **avoiding our weakness** and giving due credit of being extraordinary to competitors.

Develop a mechanism to look back honestly at your previous challenges either in your relationship, business, social or Career-related, review and try to establish the type of biases you are automated with.

System Thinking Checklist: This was the last session, and all three were thinking a clear checklist that shall define system thinking in all conditions. Astrid expressed, Dr. Hudson had explained so well conceptually and substantially, would it be right to ask for a short cut checklist in last session?

John confidently said, of course, it would be fine, Dr. Hudson; we have a common thought, that is the welfare of humankind. He knows well that we rise by lifting others and fail by failing others.

We went to Dr. Hudson for last session.

Amrit Politely requested, Dr. Hudson, we are going to take this leadership development activity to all types of strata across the globes; as a mentor, complete team of Sri Swami would always be there, but we may have some time self-doubt, mostly situational. Would you please give us a checklist of what system thinking is in all conditions?

Dr. Hudson Smiled, you people are true meaning of humanity, and I am glad to know the intention. Dr. Hudson handed over a golden plate on which a silver-written checklist was shining. Folks, this is the only set I have, so kindly note it down. We started to follow quickly.

- System thinking is a journey from Part to whole
- System thinking is a journey from self-interest to welfare for all.
- System thinking is a journey from ambiguity to clarity.
- System thinking is a journey from Indecisiveness to Decisiveness.
- System thinking is a journey from symptom to root cause

- System thinking is a journey from content to pattern
- System thinking is a journey from objective knowledge to contextual knowledge.
- System thinking is a journey from structure to process
- System Thinking is a journey to shift from Perception to Reality.

SUMMING IT UP:

➢ Leadership System thinking is 5th step of leadership Development.

➢ System thinking is a modern tool which makes the Decision process simple through refined thinking.

➢ System thinking is based on understanding the interconnectedness of different processes.

➢ **Close loop Philosophy** says generic solution without understanding system thinking is most likely to reverse.

➢ System thinking brings Clarity, Decisiveness, Problem-solving skills, understanding patterns or trends of any event, contextual knowledge and Systematic Process approach.

➢ To turn into system thinker, focus on 8 key high-impact factors: Process and System-oriented, big picture thought, strong interpersonal skill, Socialization, analytical skill, navigating complexity, lifelong learner and understanding self-biasness.

CHECK YOUR UNDERSTANDING:

- What is the good practice you see in your society that could be great to implement in your organization?

- What are the good things that you see in friends, colleagues or neighbours that could be helpful to implement in you?

- Write the 8 factors of Bricks of system thinkers, evaluate what is working great for you, and what is required to improve in you.

- Plan 10 years and beyond for your Health, Dream, Career and Financial status. Use all the possible causes which can stop or support you?

Chapter - 06

Leadership Implementation

Our Zurich Journey with Dr Hudson has given incredible insight into leadership.

We had an American Airlines flight from Zurich to Tucson, USA. Our mentor, Mr. Herald Trump, was continuously in touch with us. His voice was so deep with love that we started to gear up with high hopes. We had a two-night recreation vacation in resort in Tucson. We all three decided to meet each other after two days to give some personal time to our souls. **Our reflection is how we feel from inside; it is not physical; taking care of self, loving to self is not selfish**. It is first gate to learn how best we can serve others. If we cannot be kind and caring to ourselves, it is impossible to give our best to organizations, societies, families or any other context.

After two days of personal recreation time, our team met at lunch; we decided to review our progress and yet some of the challenges were not clear how to counter.

After detailed brain storming, we had a few questions where clarity was missing. We noted our agenda points before starting to Nogales Arizona, USA. We printed our agenda to start with our session. Monday Morning at 5AM, we started our 80 km journey to Nogales Arizona. We arrived at the address of Mr. Herald Trump. Mr. Herald, in saffron dress, was waiting on the gate of his Spiritual leader's tribe. It is one of the centres of attraction to retreat for tourists at Nogales, Arizona.

Nogales Arizona is a unique place, which spreads up to two different cities; one common name and two different countries, Nogales Arizona in north inside USA and Nogales Mexico to the south. It was an awesome trip with Mr. Herald Trump on the first evening of our stay. The only event was that in Mexico side of Arizona during our return, a dipper snatched the purse of Amrit.

First Day Session at Arizona:

We met Mr. Trump at 5AM at his Spiritual leader tribe convention centre. After meditation and Yoga, we started session.

Mr. Trump, in his passionate words, asked,

Hope you all have given enough rest to your body, mind and soul. This is the reason we have a prerequisite to spend two days with self before coming to Spiritual leader's tribe.

We greeted Mr. Trump with positive vibes.

We requested that we have a few grey areas on leadership, which is now our prime agenda for this session.

- Why are Training and Workshops not so effective and successful in producing the world-class leaders?
- Why do some leaders stand tall in front of adversities, but some fail with similar experiences and qualifications?
- How do we see potential in leaders to take organizations or societies to the next level?
- What are more important, Results, Process or something else in leadership?
- How do leaders keep motivated without getting stuck in spite of conflicts and uncertainties?

Mr. Trump saw our agenda points and smiled, these are not grey areas, dears; these are the areas which will be covered in the sessions with me. The answer to all your questions is only one. Leaders with better Spiritual Quotients can only produce world-class leaders, and this comes with continuous practice, not with training. Standing tall in adversities and looking potential in leaders are the most important aspects of leadership and leaders who are self-motivated only have one characteristic -Spiritual Quotients.

We looked at each other; this was the first time we could not understand anything.

Astrid requested: Mr. Trump, can you kindly elaborate to make it clearer?

Mr. Trump replied, it means your outer world is a reflection of your inner strength; this inner strength is beyond the five senses of organs that are your Spiritual Quotient.

Astrid politely requested: We are still not clear, Mr. Trump. This is such an important aspect; can you kindly elaborate in detail on the structure of Spiritual quotients? How does it work, and how can it strengthen this superior internal strength?

Mr. Trump, Understood Astrid, definitely, I will explain first time the structure and details of source of spiritual quotients; I will keep answering your Agenda points and additionally, I would explain the relationship between two other quotients Intelligence Quotients (IQ) and Emotional Quotients (EQ).

Now, let me go through explaining all your agenda points, all your training on leadership touches the upper part of the Tree, which contains branches and leaves. This is called crown part, but source of energy to this crown, called strength, is driven from deeper layers. The next deeper layers are in Potential/natural Talent, followed by inner strength and Spiritual strength. No training programme can activate these deeper layers unless one individual does not put in conscious self-effort. Exactly the same answers follow the question of why some leaders are successful in adversity and some fail with similar backgrounds. The stronger the deeper layer, like internal strength and spiritual strength, the more capability one has to face the situation. Mostly in all fields, leaders are evaluated on crown strengths and natural talents; however, both are the only outer layers, but source of energy is root-like inner strengths and spiritual strengths not evaluated.

Stronger root makes greater leadership ability. A tree's beauty lies in its branches, but its strength lies in its roots.

We were amazed to hear this clarity, which we had not thought of so far. Slowly, we were arriving to the point of imbibing leadership skills to practice.

Mr. Trump continued in his flow; the important question is How to see the potential in leaders. Well, we must continue to see the outer layers like strength and Potential Parts, but today, societies and corporates nearly consider 100% of the weightage of these outer layers. It must change drastically, for Potential in Leaders, outer layers like strength and potential/Natural talent shall not be weighted more than 20-40%; the rest 80-60% must be focused on inner strength and spiritual strength because even outer layer strengths cannot be sustained without getting energy from inner strengths and spiritual strength.

Mr. Trump continued in this WOW moment with silence. Let me explain one-to-one co-relation.

➤ Roots Absorb Water, Minerals, and Nutrients from soil and Transports through Xylem across the tree, similarly, your spiritual and inner strengths absorb all the nutrients which define you and transport them to your visible strengths.

➤ Roots anchor the tree in the ground and create stability, especially as a tree grows higher. Similarly, your Spiritual and inner strengths keep you grounded to not make public or private mistakes and sustain your growth.

➤ Stronger Roots keep trees grounded in heavy storm co-relation so that your Spiritual and inner strengths mentor you to navigate in the tough times.

Unfortunately, in societies, organisations and even in personal life, the storm of volatility, uncertainty, complexity and ambiguity is a day-to-day endeavour, so activated Inner and Spiritual strengths must be on autopilot to navigate you.

Compromised root systems from root diseases are major reasons we see trees failing. Similarly, compromised Inner and spiritual strengths are major reasons for our unfulfillment.

It was now late evening, and with dinner, we finished the sessions of first day. We were charged with titillation of today's crystal-clear session. We all had a similar feeling to spend some time with self to rethink our strengths.

Second Day Session at Arizona:

We started 2nd day from the point we stopped; after warm-up session, Mr. Trump quickly jumped to the subject.

One more aspect is for leadership, what is important Result or process? I would say neither is most important. Process is preferred over result. When you are building societies, communities, Businesses or communicable qualities in individuals, it must have long-term factors. Considering long-term view, Input and by-products are more important. Evaluation of input and by-Products is always done and taken in right spirit by inner strength and spiritual strengths. The Case study of Rise and Fall of General Electric is very famous across the globe.

During the tenure of Chairman and chief executive Mr. John F. 'Jack' Welch Jr, GE excelled in every field. Prior to that, GE was already the most successful organisation in USA for products ranging from light bulbs, Television, washing machines, electric stoves, electric automotive and locomotives, X-ray Machines, various medical equipment and home appliances; the culture of organisation was known as PICTIC. This **P**rogressive, **I**nnovative, **C**onnected, **T**ransparent, **I**nclusive and **C**ollaborative culture was the by-product of previous leadership. It was the unique culture of GE, which had seen consistent growth from 1892 to 1981. GE was no more the same under Mr. Jack Welch. His policy to fire the lowest 10% performer every year brought an infamous name for him, Neutron Jack' Welch. But this policy made many managers insecure, and transparency and collaborative approach were not the same inside the company. The concept is same as an employee's Spiritual strength misaligned from outer layer in the game of survival. Mr Jack Welch focused on short-term performance; GE acquired financial services and NBCs, which was only meant for making money rather than core innovative services.

Market capital of GE increased from $14 billion to more than $410 billion during Welch's tenure, and Revenue grew nearly five times. Welch's team was instrumental in managing and manipulating financial data to project continuous growth. This greed spoiled company culture and transparency. Principle was very clear; get numbers at any cost. This was the input to run the GE business. Now, look at how at that time Welch was assessed.

Fortune magazine called Welch as "Manager of the Century" and "The Ultimate Manager".

Countless companies copied his result-oriented approach and in late 2008, he started to regret it after diluting company culture. If you relook carefully, Jack Welch was great on his outer layer strength and Potential; this shows how he managed numbers kept going, but he was not good enough in inner and Spiritual strength. Socialise for purpose of all is one characteristic of inner strength, which means a high spiritual quotient person shall not cause harm to surroundings but fire 10% of the lowest performing employees. Even those employees may not be actually lowest performing because of a lack of transparency.

Astrid asked a question - This time, you used Spiritual Quotient, how does it belong here?

Mr. Trump smiled, good observation, Astrid, I mean with Spiritual Quotient. I will explain this in another session.

Now, connect to the point of GE's business process. A few things are very clear in analysis.

- Nearly 48% of profit of GE was contributed by GE Capital, a financial wing not from core sectors.

- Obviously, Top performers were always from financial wing of GE Capital, and most fired employees were core experts who were innovative and prudent on industrial products but not so good at managing numbers. It impacted and further worsened the core sectors of business.

- Assessing the Financial wing and core product sectors, which were proven and sustained for 80 years on the same parameter, was not an inclusive approach.

- Jack Welch's image was created more by media because in the same period of 80s and 90s, S&P 500 grew at the same speed the way GE grew. The fastest growth registered by GE between 1994 and 2000 when Bull Run was at its peak in USA. it is more about the scenario of "**Rising tide lifts all ships**".

- GE capital was strategically inducted into GE's Business process without good intentions. Everything that GE produced was leased, rented, or loaned by GE Capital on higher interest; many vendors of GE's core business, many retail dealers, etc., were recommended or forced to follow that. It ruined the complete credibility of the company and GE's capital time projected profit at the cost of internal business of GE's core sector.

GE case study and, like many such business growth and downfall stories, fit the tree model.

SQ EQ and IQ Tree model: In an ideal situation, human total quotients must have the below tree structure model. A strong Spiritual quotient of leaders and managers keeps a high level of intelligence and Emotional quotient.

For leaders to sustain and consistently stand tall in face of challenges, install inner strength through self-reflection.

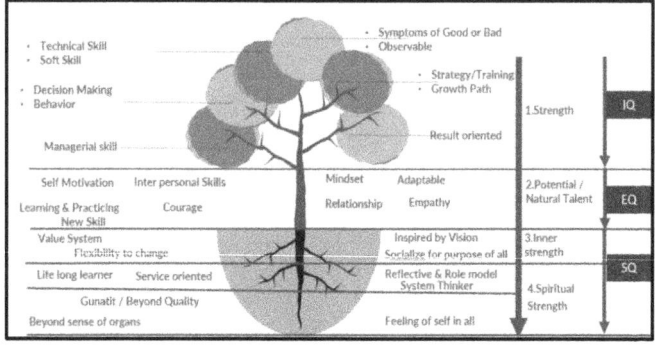

Spiritual quotient has two layers.

Total spiritual quotients = Inner strengths +Spiritual strength

Folks, Mr. Trump continued, -let's understand deeply this master skill to transform individuals. We had nothing to ask or get clarified. We were landed into totally unknown territory.

Intelligence Quotient, which is very much visible, is easiest to install with little more effort and clarity. It is all about attention, logic, analytical skill, behaviour factors, etc., one to gather, process and analyse information effectively.

IQ Enhanced ideation, focus, strategic thought, ability to learn-relearn

Managing emotions is more important than managing your intellect. Hence the next layer of your tree model is Emotional Quotient.

Emotional Quotient develops by coupling living in present and observing carefully yourself and your surroundings. How well do we know ourselves and our fellow human beings, including how we feel, why we feel that way, what motivates us, and how to use that knowledge to the benefit of individuals, organizations, and societies? The key factors of EQ include self-motivation, interpersonal skills, Mindset, Relationship management, adaptability, Empathy, Courage, Learning and practicing new Skills, etc.

Researchers Goleman, Boyatzis and McKee analysed year's data from close to 500 competence models from global companies, including the likes of IBM, Lucent, PepsiCo, British Airways, and academic institutions and different government agencies. To determine which capabilities drove outstanding performance in these organisations, they grouped capabilities into 3 categories: 1) Technical 2) Cognitive 3) EQ (Emotional Quotients).

After analysing all the data, they found that EQ-based competencies played an increasingly important role at higher levels of organisation, where differences in technical skills are of negligible importance. Moreover, about 85% of the difference in star-performers profiles from average-performers was attributable to EQ-related factors.

Now, the question is how to develop strong and sustainable emotional quotients. Do we have some Process?

To be surprised, John, only ancient Indian wisdom and medieval Japan had an answer to this. Mr. Trump had a big pause here. Perhaps he had regretted learning it too late.

Emotional Quotient had a deep relationship to get strengthened by another layer shown in tree model as Spiritual Quotient. Like Jack Welch, he had good Intelligence Quotient; he understood his surroundings well, had good coordination between different stakeholders in GE entities, managed motivation, had the courage to make decisions, etc., overall, he had good Emotional Quotient. What he was missing - Spiritual Quotient. What Jack was lacking - Value system on which GE had excelled for many decades.

He was lacking Inspired by vision, Reflective system thinking and purpose of all.

Long-time CEO Jeff Immelt was saddled with the doomed legacy of the previous CEO, Jack Welch.

General Electric had been spoiled by greed, lack of transparency, and "lax oversight and buried risks."

The symptom was Welch's forceful, numbers-obsessed management style. This is the reason Spiritual Quotients are the most important for Leaders serving communities, Organisations and Societies. It is easily possible to get self-obsessed, like Welch in spite of having Good IQ and EQ.

How SQ Works and Development Process:

Meditation: Regular practice of meditation can help individuals connect with their inner selves and develop a deeper understanding of their self.

Meditation is a scientifically proven process to enhance your spiritual quotients and foster high value and flexibility. This flexibility comes primarily from Spiritual quotient that helps leaders understand better people from different back. The relationships at the workplace keep on shifting and changing due to the numerous people around and also because people come and go. The outlook, working style, thought process, manner of working and everything else differ from person to person, which requires a level of flexibility and adaptability.

Mindfulness: Practicing mindfulness involves being present and fully engaged in the present moment without judgment. This can help individuals develop a greater sense of inner peace and calm. Mindfulness enhances long-term vision in leaders and decision-making process.

Self-reflection: Taking time for self-reflection and introspection can help individuals gain a deeper understanding of their values, beliefs, and purpose in life.

Practicing Gratitude and Compassion: Practicing gratitude involves cultivating a sense of appreciation and thankfulness for the good things in life, which can help individuals develop a positive and optimistic outlook.

Practicing compassion involves developing empathy and understanding for others, which can help individuals develop a deeper sense of connection with others and the world around them.

Gratitude and compassion are unconscious elements that you must start slowly to practice and integrate with you to activate your spiritual quotients.

It simply means seeing "World as a natural extension of self". This will increase your generosity of spirit and will take away distractions of spiritual quotients like ego, fear, laziness, blaming and complaining attitudes.

Service: Engaging in service to others can help individuals connect with their spiritual nature and develop a sense of purpose and meaning in life.

You will understand the meaning of happiness for different human beings; turning absolute givers into societies, Communities or organisation is one of the highest rated qualities of leadership which gets developed here. Another **big quality you imbibe in your spiritual quotient is ability to bounce back during setbacks**.

Mindful communication: Practicing mindful communication involves being present and fully engaged in conversations with others, listening deeply and speaking authentically. This can help individuals build deeper, more meaningful connections with others and develop a greater sense of spiritual fulfilment.

Reading Great Books: Reading great books and practicing the concepts from those books synergise you. It integrates your spirit with your body, which produces alignment between truly you and what you do. Reading books makes you more expressive, which helps you practice gratitude and compassion. When you read the different books, your inner development has been mentored by different methodologies. Learning these different concepts for your growth and development, you learn the valuing adversity, which is an important outcome of good spiritual quotients.

SUMMING IT UP:

➢ Leadership Implementation is 6th step of leadership Development.

➢ Our reflection is how we feel from inside; it is not physical. Taking care of self and loving to self is not selfish.

➢ This step solves the important challenges of leadership like why Training does not work in leadership development, why with the same qualifications, one leader succeeds and other does not, how to keep motivated in uncertainties, etc.

➢ Spiritual quotients in leadership are most important transferes energy for consistency to Strengths (IQ) and Potentials (EQ)

- Spiritual quotient is explained for simplicity as tree Model. Spiritual quotient is like Root, Emotional quotient is like Trunk, Branches and Leaves are like Intelligence Quotient.
- Understand each component from tree model to enhance your required skills.
- Value system, flexibility to change, inspired by vision, lifelong learner, service-oriented, and System thinkers are parameters of Spiritual quotients.
- For activating spiritual quotients, which every human has a few good practices, like Meditation, practicing Gratefulness and compassion, Service-oriented attitude and reading great books must be developed.

CHECK YOUR UNDERSTANDING:

- Sit in a calm place and think about a few questions like:
- Who am I? Why am I in this world doing this activity?
- What are the IQ and EQ characteristics you are good at? (Refer to Characteristics from Tree model)
- What are Spiritual quotient characteristics you are good at?
- How many activities do you perform consistently from the SQ development essentials?

➤ Why do you get stressed? Why do you fear or feel anxiety at work place?

➤ Do you respect diversity or views which do not align with you? Write why or why not.

Chapter - 07

Brand Leadership Management

We landed at Indira Gandhi International airport on 18th June 2023. On 21st June, we were the part of International Yoga Day celebration at Assi Ghat, Varanasi, along with Sri Swami. Again, we connected to our soul which was important learning. Next day, we met Sri Swami just after the divine morning Vandana and felt the warmth of his calmness and compassion when he was serving the food to cows and crows. In today's volatile world, when Humans are busy snatching food from each other in the game of power, position and social status, it is striking for leadership dimension to extend up to animals. Now, we realised one thing that we started to catch the trends. Our observation had gone to the micro level, and conclusions from observations are more purposeful. The change with leadership excellence within you to see same thing differently because you have your window clean.

Sri Swami smiled and hugged us in corporate style, folks, you all did a dazzlingly smooth execution; your profound changes are visible to me.

Sri Swami asked gracefully, how was your Leadership learning? We all looked at each other. Perhaps we could not decide who should start and on what topic.

Sri Swami said, this is the next step of your leadership; here clarity goes to its peak. This is a common problem in all organisations, societies and communities we see. How do you coordinate and collaborate? The Idea of sending four different leaders was to send a clear message: Individually, we are one drop, but Together, we are an ocean. To create a strong value, you must see someone else's strength as a complement to your weakness and not a threat to your position or authority. All the trainers were initially trained by me in the same Leadership Club. All had specific strengths, so we aligned on the training subjects.

The core strengths to communicate are connecting and conquering together.

Incredible message, Sri Swami, Astrid said.

We would like to take a 15-minute break before the summary of learning - Astrid requested.

That is perfectly fine; I loved this approach; making informed decision is good sign of mature leaders.

We used the inner strength and natural alignment method for Summary. We quickly returned with better alignment. Very quick, great, folks.

John started, Thanks Sri Swami; after a strong clarity on why, during the session with you, we visited Thirumalaisamudram to Meet Susamya.

The learning from Susamya is foundation of our leaders' thoughts. She explained the four cycles in the way of becoming a leader: Purpose cycle, Productive cycle, Habit cycle and self-balancing.

Each cycle has three Sub-steps, and hence, a total of 12 steps are required to focus on to start with leadership. But we mostly were doing on Finance and personal aspects. This was the foundation that awakened us from the core.

Yes, John the great, those 12 steps are worth writing on Golden paper and seeing every day that you can review your progress.

John continues, Yes, Sri Swami, these pre-requisites are first step towards leadership. The challenge of leadership is to be strong but not rude; be kind but not weak; be bold but not bully; be thoughtful but not lazy; be humble but not timid; be proud but not arrogant; have humour but without folly.

Miles ahead, my kid, Sri Swami's eyes sparked like Parents on the success of Kids.

John handed over to Astrid smoothly, and she started gracefully, Sri Swami, I would be taking Charge of learning from Dr. Hudson. With this amazing mentor, we learnt an important concept. We started with you on "Our Why". We learnt from Susamya what leaders should have stuff with why in this volatile world. Dr. Hudson taught us how leaders must think, and hence System thinking is the new way of thinking.

Close-loop system concept to solve the problems is amazing to avoid shortcuts to solve the problems; Bricks of System thinker's is a systematic approach with details of all eight elements to turn into system thinkers.

Sri Swami complimented; True, the writer Peter Senge says, "Systems thinking is a discipline for seeing wholes. It is a framework for seeing interrelationships rather than things, for seeing 'patterns of change' rather than 'static snapshots."

Yes, Sri Swami, from a leader's point of view, this is worth understanding; Leaders contribute to societies, Communities, organisations and Nations. Understanding interconnectedness will ensure a safer and more responsible world. They do not only decide on careers, Regulations or businesses. Decisions on individuals connect to family, societies and sometimes nations. Assassination of Archduke Ferdinand, the immediate reason for the first world war was taken by a leader, but interconnectedness led to millions of losses of life, generations were impacted badly, and human saw not only one but two world wars. This must be in thought process of leaders.

Lovely, you beat my expectation, my daughter. Sri Swami touched her head in blessed touch.

Astrid stared at Amrit with Gentle smile, indicating, it is your turn. It was a superb transition of role.

Amrit started; I must express my deepest gratitude to you to introduce us to great source of learning. Arizona is fabulous location; though our start was bit scary, it was exactly started from the place, Dr. Hudson signed off. With Dr. Hudson, we learned about System thinking and how to turn a system thinker. Mr. Trump taught us what the layers within us are, who refines this thought process and gives us power to execute, sustain and face challenges. It was nothing less than a bible of layers of leadership quality within us. This was the session of the process of making a genuine, strong and scientific leader. The Four layers, like,

Strength = Intelligence Quotient

Potential /Natural talent = Emotional Quotients

Inner Strength = Spiritual Quotient

Inner strength +Spiritual strength = Spiritual Quotient

Sri Swami remarked with grace, yes, I heard about snatching incidents on Mexico side of Arizona, Amrit. Indeed, it is a good lesson; both sides of Arizona's people shares common culture, DNA and customs. In every scientific way, they are same. Yet Mexico side of Arizona has a huge poverty, more crime, less industrialization and less literacy rate because USA side had access to great systems where people grow together. People are taken care of by law makers. **We are less a product of our culture and more a product of leadership associated with.**

Amrit started again, this was such a precious lesson which cleared our doubt about why some leaders stay tall in face of adversity, and some with similar backgrounds give up. Our strength lies in inner strength and spiritual strength. This spiritual quotient must be active and strengthened as a leader.

Sri Swami, mind-boggling Amrit, you all made my day. Each one of you had gone a mile ahead to learn these leadership skills.

With these lessons, do you think your purpose to visit met?

We all replied univocal, sure. Now, we have enough confidence that we can make the tribe change the situation on the science of people.

Great, but one step is still remaining, which will be most important.

Sri Swami asked, what are the ultimate stage and phase of leadership?

John replied, we understand that excellence in our function of work is the ultimate stage and phase.

During this process, we learn a lot and expand ourselves with learning.

Sri Swami, advanced the discussion, learning and expansion are part of the Journey; that is perfectly right, dearest john, but how do you measure the excellence in your work?

Subtle observation was a way of thinking of Sri Swami; we all are admired.

Sri Swami took a deep breath and continued, John, do you remember, you had a question, "What is brand leadership?" during our conversation on Stanford University and Fredrick Terman.

John replied with grace, yes, Sri Swami, and you parked this question for later part of the time.

Sri Swami replied with amazing calmness and enthusiasm, yes John, and this is the right time.

I used Brand leadership for Fredrick Terman because he envisioned beyond expectation; he is called by many as the Father of Silicon Valley. He was dean of Stanford University. His idea to establish Stanford Industrial Park is even today being implemented by universities and companies for mutual benefit. It provides an edge to engineering graduates to know the industrial practices, and Industry gets fresh talents. Soon, many laboratories, technology centres and research centres were flooded in Stanford by Eastman Kodak, General Electric, Preformed Line Products, Admiral Corporation, Shockley Transistor Laboratory of Beckman Instruments, Lockheed, Hewlett-Packard, and many others.

Even today, all great companies, like Adobe, Google, Meta, Apple, Wells Fargo, Visa, Intel, Lockheed Martin, Cisco and many more giants who are disrupting the lives of Millions, are from Silicon Valley.

Brand Leaders leave the footprint beyond the timeline. They connect humanity; at least, their thoughts and actions follow this direction.

Blue Print of Brand Leadership: Folks, in the below diagram, we have summarised all the characteristics of Brand Leaders.

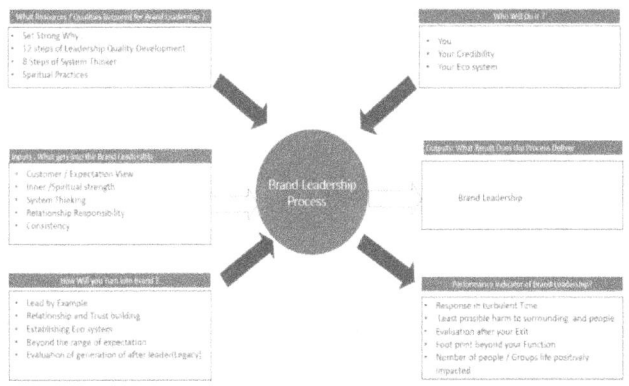

We say blueprint because this is the ultimate stage of leadership. This stage enjoys the members of all greats like Mahatma Gandhi, Mandela, Swami Vivekanand and Albert Einstein.

It also has a long list of lesser-known social workers who served thousands being selfless, like mountain man Dashrath Manjhi from India, who made the way through mountain individually to support villagers.

Now is the right time to understand the deeper thought of leadership. Brand leadership is popular, maybe sometimes position also and most of the time public figure. It is a stage of a journey, but leadership is not at all related to Position, Power or Authority. Some people hold high positions and authority and are not at all leaders, but someone may be a common person in the lowest ladder of Position and authority can be absolutely a leader.

Input of Brand Leaders: Turning into brand leaders is a consistent journey. After studying the key common characteristics of leadership Clubs:

Observed followings are strongly embedded:

- Customer /Expectation view
- Inner /Spiritual strength
- System Thinking
- Relationship Responsibilities
- Consistency

How will you turn into brand leadership?

- Lead by Example
- Complete responsibility for relationship and trust-building
- Establishing Ecosystem
- Beyond the range of expectation (diversified contribution)
- Legacy beyond timeline

Performance indicators of brand leaders:

- Response in a turbulent time
- Least possible harm to surrounding and people
- Evaluation after your Exit
- Footprint beyond your function
- Number of people/ groups positively impacted.

This is simplified and crisp, Sri Swami, Amrit said. Just a few questions are looming,

How do Brand leaders handle success?

Handling success by Brand Leaders:

Folks, Brand leader's success is the success of people. Brand leaders are not self-centric; they know the clear difference between how they feel and how they handle their feelings. Brand leaders have skill to make other people feel important. They might be major stakeholder of success, but they claim if something is left. After each success, brand leaders do not evaluate on basis of what is in it for me, but they evaluate what I contributed. They are absolutely givers. They do not blame the situation but find the path; it becomes a deep-rooted habit of finding the solution. When India was not so conducive for businessmen, then visionary industrialist, JRD Tata said, "I do not want India to be an economic superpower. I want India to be a happy country."

Business, relationships, education, politics, sports, wealth, and sometimes, even war, they all have the only purpose for brand leaders to bring enduring happiness and prosperity.

Brand Leaders are system Thinkers and possess all the interconnectedness. They see big picture through skill of system thinking and come out with creative solutions and, most of the time, are decisive. Optimism and positive thinking make them resilient to all the risks in their surroundings.

Five Habits of Brand Leadership: These habits are worth practicing and, over a period of time, will be integrated into auto-pilot mode.

High Energy and Resilience level: They keep up their energy level with the control of all possible distractions, practicing meditation exercises, healthy lifestyle and positive thoughts. With practice of all leadership steps, knowingly or unknowingly, they turn highly resilient to not wear out in tough conditions, and if happens so, they quickly bounce back.

High Spiritual Quotients: Brand leaders possess most of the qualities like clear purpose, deeper meaning of life, Gratitude and compassion, service-oriented thought, etc.

L2L Connectivity: Leaders to Leader connectivity is being socialised with like-minded people for a common purpose. Brand leaders develop and grow multi-fold connections. It provides understanding and learning relationship challenges.

Feedback to Feedforward: It is not the case that Brand leaders always do everything right. Brand leaders develop a belief system that everything, even in the best situation, has scope for improvement. With this belief system, they always gather the feedback to understand that the work, service or activity performed by them is helping people in right context. Today, feedback is a customary practice, and people do not really take action on feedback but brand leaders are different. They take the proper action, and they believe,

"People learn more deeply and remember things better when they have found the answer to a problem themselves." This is how they evolve utilising feedback. Turning feedback into action for continual growth and development is feedforward.

Mentoring and Journaling: Brand leaders upgrade themselves through continuous mentoring. They also will keep journaling their idea to keep the flow intact with themselves. Journaling deepens self-discovery, a communicational channel for self. Journaling helps brand leaders take a leap to next steps. Noted German Diarist wrote that "I can shake off everything as I write; my sorrows disappear, my courage is reborn."

SUMMING IT UP:

- Brand leadership Management is 7th step of leadership Development.

- This is elite stage of rare leadership; it needs very long-term conscious effort. The purpose to explain here is to start imbibing these qualities in small baby steps.

- We are less a product of our culture and more a product of leadership associated with it.

- Focus from turtle diagram on Input of Brand Leadership, what resources are required and how you will turn into Brand leader.

- Brand leaders establish ecosystem and they leave footprint beyond timeline.

- Bring the 5 habits of Brand leaders in yourself.

CHECK YOUR UNDERSTANDING:

- How do you collaborate with Team when you have to brief about activities performed as Team?

- ➤ What are performance indicators of brand leadership matche you and why?
- ➤ What are the Brand leadership habits you follow?

Chapter - 08

Conclusion

"Endings are the doorway to the next beginning." - Patricia Cornwell.

After returning from Varanasi, we started a leadership awareness and leadership development activity through leadership club.

We systematically organised our learning and started a flagship program, **"Seven Steps of Leadership Journey"**. Our purpose of transforming individuals was moving in the right direction. We were getting great support from all our mentors, Susmya, Dr. Hudson, Mr. Trump and Sri Swami. Things started to change over a period of time due to some essential priorities. We were still committed to showing the light of leadership out of dark tunnels of challenges. John and Astrid married and settled in the farmhouse of Dr. Hudson to advance the well-being leadership movement. Amrit asked for support from Sriswami, who suggested Amrit take the help of an author to write the details of your leadership journey in a book to make it available for all who have strong passion for changing the world around them.

Personal note and Final Though from Author:

Dear Readers,

This book I have written with some clear vision and purpose after reading more than 150 powerful business and management books, and interacting with more than 200 CEOs of medium and large-scale industries, who started from nothing many years before. Few things I clearly understood.

- Many self-helps books touch in details one aspect of learning but not most of the essentials. Though not in detail, I have tried to bring all essential ingredients to turn into leaders in a single place.

- Leadership skill is long-term continual, deliberate effort as Leadership learner explores as many possible practical aspects.

- In Interaction with all the Leaders, one common trait I observed they all got transformed with handling challenges. Every challenge in your life has come to transform you; face it with iron finch.

- Human essential needs are same for all; we need happiness, Peace of mind, improved health, well-placed flow of energy, etc. These Essentials are contagious. If we need happiness, we must not make people unreasonably unhappy. If we need good heath, we must not create unhealthy environments for others.

- For Development process, the most important two aspects are: **First Start** even with nothing, and **second have consistency**. Good system and Process of fast learning will come over a period of time. Your start is not expected to be great. Think about yourself when you write first alphabetical letter; think about your first day of school, leaving behind your parents; horrible, right! Like leadership, perfection is the greatest friend of consistency.

- You are your biggest friend, and you are your biggest enemy. You have a choice to decide what you want to become if you start polishing worry, jealousy, anger, stress, anxiety and negative stuff. The first thing it will attack is your energy level and your health. These are your enemy. If you start polishing gratefulness, compassion, love and positive thought, the first thing it will benefit is your focus on peak performance and good health.

- No books can give you readymade solutions to all your Challenges. That is why each one of us has a unique journey. What is important to give mental diet to develop resilience is to not wear out and learn the process of facing challenges. No stone will turn a great statue without facing a chisel, and no ornament of gold will shine without melting and purification process. Get ready to embark on your journey with challenges.

- As you Read and reflect on these leadership qualities, please share your thoughts and motivate people around you. Leadership is one skill which is the biggest gift you can offer to your near and dear ones.

- Socializing is the biggest way to test your leadership skills. You may not always be as per your will. You may feel that the leadership qualities that you are applying are not at all being reflected by others, and you are a loser with all great qualities. These are practical constraints, but believe the process; it will work. Only in practical sense, some strategic alignment will be required. It will teach you collaboration and teamwork.

May this book equip you with the tools for leadership.

Best Wishes from
Lakshmi Narayan Pandey
Commonly known in close circle
Narayan Swami

www.ingramcontent.com/pod-product-compliance
Lightning Source LLC
LaVergne TN
LVHW061547070526
838199LV00077B/6931